Media & Democracy

Media & Democracy

edited by

Everette E. Dennis
Robert W. Snyder

Transaction Publishers
New Brunswick (U.S.A.) and London (U.K.)

Library of Congress Catalog Number: 97–23126
ISBN: 0–7658–0408–5
Printed in the United States of America

Library of Congress Cataloging-in-Publication Data

Media and democracy / edited by Everette E. Dennis and Robert W. Snyder.
    p. cm.—(Media studies series)
  Originally published in the summer 1995 issue of Media studies journal.
  Includes bibliographical references and index.
  ISBN 0–7658–0408–5 (pbk. : alk. paper)
  1. Mass media—Political aspects. 2. Democracy. 3. Freedom of the press. 4. Journalism—Political aspects. 5. Mass media—Technological innovations. I. Dennis, Everette E. I. Snyder, Robert W., 1955–
III. Series.
P95.8.M387   1997
302.23—dc21   97–23126
                                                   CIP

Contents

Part I: Definitive Questions

An author, media scholar and former Media Studies Center senior fellow explains why the media are not, inherently, agents of democracy. "Mass media can serve democracy only when those who manage them feel a passionate responsibility to create it and maintain it."

Market and technological forces are altering the role of the media in public life, argues a professor of communications at the University of Amsterdam and former Media Studies Center senior fellow. "Whether one is a pessimist or an optimist, there is little doubt that things are changing fundamentally and a reassessment of the media-politics relationship is high on the agenda for those who care about democracy."

Part II: Media and the Dynamics of Democracy Around the World

"For the past two centuries, it was *law* that provided the source of authority for democracy. Today, law seems to be replaced by *opinion* as the source of authority, and the media serve as the arbiters of public opinion." In this new situation, the former secretary-general of the United Nations makes a firm commitment to press freedom.

The president of the Czech Republic considers the importance of a free press, responsibility and cultural standards. "In its own way, the press—as a part of the information and communication system of today's civilization—is a soul of the soul of all mankind. It is a medium of self-understanding."

The power of the press is closely related to democracy, writes a professor of communication and sociology at the University of California, San Diego and former Media Studies Center fellow. "The news gains power not in its direct impact on audiences but in the belief, justified in viable democracies, that the knowledge of citizens can from time to time be effective."

The Chinese Communist Party is introducing market economics while maintaining control in the political realm, writes a veteran China watcher, now dean of the University of California's Graduate School of Journalism. "But just as the pressure of one geologic plate against another creates earthquakes, it is possible that China's increasingly market-driven media will ultimately collide with its stubbornly resistant, Leninist state in a politically tectonic way."

Market reforms and satellite television have transformed Indian broadcasting, writes the television critic for *The Hindu* in New Delhi, India. But there is a price: "Television, which was started in India to remedy underdevelopment, is now preoccupied with commercial broadcasting."

In the '90s, writes a *Wall Street Journal* reporter who has covered Africa since 1986, African nations have intensified efforts to establish market economies and multiparty democracies. "Growing pains, however, including squabbles over press freedom, will continue to be part of the process."

As nations struggle to build democracies and market economies, journalists wrestle with everything from censorship to bringing down governments. "In the land of magic realism everything can happen," notes a writer for *Clarín* of Buenos Aires, Argentina—"hell and utopia alike."

In the old world of communism, writes the editor in chief of Poland's *Gazeta Wyborcza*, the difference between good and evil was as clear as the contrast between black and white. "In the world of democracy, the prevailing color is gray. This world is ruled by arguments which are divided and not complete, by partial and contradictory interests."

The mayor of Budapest, Hungary—a former *samizdat* publisher—explores the growing appreciation of free expression in Eastern Europe. "I take this as the safest guarantee of the demise of censorship, which is destined to become a phenomenon so irrelevant that in the future it will arouse only the interest of media historians."

In the countries of the former Soviet Union a distinctly different view of press freedom has emerged, argues a communications law scholar. "In the emerging battle for identities in Ukraine or Kazakhstan, Estonia or Azerbaijan, independence has often meant, above all, freedom from televised images produced by Russia."

Since the collapse of communism in Eastern Europe, Americans have ventured abroad to spread their journalistic gospel. The dean of the Manship School of Mass Communication and former president of the Center for Foreign Journalists offer suggestions. "Foreign media assistance requires a long-term view. Patience, not a quick fix, will make the difference."

Part III: Journalism as a Democratic Discipline

Journalists will regain some dignity if they stop thinking of themselves as members of the media, argues the veteran broadcaster and author. "We are what we call ourselves. And for 40 years I have been proud to call myself a journalist. I think media stinks!"

The power of the media must be exercised fairly, writes the former prime minister of Canada. "No leader who has seen responsible public policy initiatives subverted or smothered by mountains of trivia and drivel and trash will disagree with the notion that perseverance in the face of indignity is one of the fundamental requirements of modern leadership."

In a personal interview, the scholar Jürgen Habermas explains to the *The Nation*'s publisher and editorial director the purpose of critical opinion magazines: "At the core of their mission is to maintain the discursive character of public communication. Who else, if not this type of press, is going to set the standards?"

The former editor of the *Wichita* (Kan.) *Eagle* explores the roots and purpose of public journalism. "Its objective is to find ways for journalism to serve a purpose beyond—but not in place of—telling the news: the purpose of reinvigorating public life by re-engaging people in it."

How should journalists in a democracy write about the past? A professor of social ethics at Union Theological Seminary and former Media Studies Center senior fellow offers suggestions. "Their goal should be to remember the past with the fullness, accuracy and empathy that prevent people from stereotyping one another and thus perpetuating their mutual enmity."

Niche marketing and new information technologies will "enhance occupational and economic opportunities," writes the former publisher of the *Oakland Tribune*. "Potential social impacts are less clear. This boon for the market may result in lousy social policy if it causes enclaves to dominate our political structure to the exclusion of a common national vision."

"Owners and investors have a right to make money," writes a professor and former dean of the Graduate School of Public Affairs at the University of Washington and former Media Studies Center senior fellow. "But has it gone too far? Are the First Amendment and professional ideals now being endangered by the drive for increased profits?"

Why are journalists so unpopular? An ABC television producer and an editor at *WORLDBusiness* provide some explanations. "People want explanations—but they want explanations that confirm their general assumptions about the way the world works, reinforce the facts they already know and uphold the beliefs they cherish."

Part IV: Democracy and New Media

Interactive telecommunications are changing politics and government, argues the president of the PBS Horizons Cable Network and former Media Studies Center senior fellow. "In the electronic republic, it will no longer be the press but the public that functions as the nation's powerful Fourth Estate, alongside the executive, the legislative and the judiciary."

"Fears that on-line media will render obsolete traditional forms of communication are unrealistic," writes a scholar at Tufts University. "On-line services could enable a greater realization of principles like equal access to information and freedom of expression, both of which are commonly associated with a sound democracy."

The Internet does not threaten American journalism, argues the author, a professor in the Graduate School of Public Affairs at the University of Washington. "Rather than dismiss new media as interlopers, journalists should seize the opportunities they provide to enrich and to extend the best of journalistic practice."

In Toronto, Citytv's "Speakers Corner" uses a video kiosk to give ordinary viewers a chance to get on the air. Moses Znaimer, founder of Citytv, calls it "unmediated," a "rough and real alternative" to the "slick, prepackaged" media content of the United States.

Part V: Books

A Canadian media scholar explores works on the media and democratic discourse. "The complaint is not simply that these enormous agencies of public address are being squandered on trivia and titillation when they could well be instruments of social betterment. Rather, as almost everyone who thinks seriously about the matter agrees, it's that they are actively making us all dumber. Right and left differ only on whether this is inadvertent or structurally convenient."

Preface

A few years ago, it might have seemed that the role and function of the mass media in a democracy were settled. After all, there were two basic functionsæthose being the free flow of information and the interplay of opinion. And, of course, citizens were guaranteed full rights of free expression. It was also assumed that both the issuer of communication (that is the press or media system) and the consumer (the citizen or public) enjoyed these rights. Arguments occasionally pitted individual rights of free expression against institutional rights and were debated in government bodies and courts. Fundamentally, though, most people understood instinctively that the media played a seminal, even central, role in the democracy and the democratic state.

For example, students of media and democracy could look to the United States, Western Europe and democracies elsewhere in the world and they could contrast these models with those of various authoritarian and communist states. Indeed, the role of media in democracy was defining in distinguishing the East-West divide during the Cold War.

As the Cold War ended and the machinery of authoritarian rule and command economies were dismantled in country after country, declarations about democratic media abounded. Before long, all but a few countries (China and North Korea being major exceptions) professed democratic values and began to redefine the role of the press in their societies. For the first time in generations, citizens and leaders discussed the ideal relationship between media and government, the nature of journalism and the definition of journalists and other media people. New press laws, some more tolerant than others, were enacted and new media systems were put in place.

Concurrent with the political and social upheaval that accompanied the end of the Cold War was the rise of the information and communication revolution. Thanks to technological progress, economic realities and more flexible legal and regulatory systems the world over, the role of media in democracy came to mean not just the traditional means of communication, but the domain of cyberspace as well. Where scarcity was once the order of the day, abundance represented in formulations of the information superhighway, expanding cable channel capacity and the infinite extensions of digital communication, changed both the contours of communication and its presumed power and reach.

Defining the role of the media in democracy now requires hard thought and new formulations. Old assumptions are no longer enough to explain what is happening in so many different societies, all saying they are democratic, but carrying out their social compact in quite different ways.

In such a time, there is value in revisiting media and democracy by searching for new definitions, examining the special mandate of journalism and public affairs coverage in this new era and by considering the special place of new media. That is what we try to do in this book, which began as an issue of the *Media Studies Journal* during my watch as founding executive director of the Media Studies Center at Columbia University. With the considerable help of this volume's co-editor, Robert W. Snyder, now editor of the *Journal*, we commissioned articles and essays by leaders and commentators from government, the media and the academy. Most of the work here was specifically written for us, while a few pieces are taken from books prepared by fellows at the Media Studies Center. Only two or three exemplary items are from previously published works. Together, we believe that they add up to a contemporary and telling examination of democratic media at the end of one century and at the dawn of another. Some pieces are global in scope and outlook, while others zero in on specific regions and countries, accounting for many conditions that fly under the democratic banner these days. It is hoped that the essays that follow, some of them passionate and persuasive accounts from players in the democratic marketplace, others the musings of scholars, encourage a serious reconceptualization of mediaæmass and personalæin the post-cold war era when expansive thinking and new formulations are so badly needed.

I am grateful to all who helped in the assembly of this volumeæco-editor Snyder and *Journal* colleagues Lisa DeLisle, Jennifer Kelley and Lauren Aaronson, as well as my assistants Cate Dolan and Stephan Wilson. This volume also benefited from a roundtable that included

Alan Brinkley and Robert Shapiro of Columbia University; John Phillip Santos of the Ford Foundation; James Clad, Georgetown University; and Monroe E. Price, Cardozo School of Law. Especially helpful to me were conversations over several years on fact-finding trips to Eastern Europe, Latin America and East Asia with Jon Vanden Heuvel, my co-author on several monographs on media and democracy in those regions, now in investment banking at Credit Suisse First Boston in New York.

Everette E. Dennis
Distinguished Visiting Professor of Communication
Graduate School of Business
Fordham University at Lincoln Center
New York City
September 1997

Introduction

While there is nearly universal agreement that the media play a vital and defining role in democracy everywhere it exists, ironically they are often unpopular. The hectoring cry of critics is, "Who elected you anyway?" To which the obvious answer is "no one," backed by the probably accurate assumption that collectively and individually the media would have a hard time winning public approval in an election.

At the same time, the media in a democratic system must be credible and reliable lest they lose their influence and authority. And it is usually acknowledged that democracy almost never flourishes without an effective, independent media.

This book, which began as an issue of the *Media Studies Journal,* takes up "Media and Democracy," with the clear recognition that generalizing about the media is often perilous.

In the years since the end of the Cold War, as democratic governments have become the order of the day in many former socialist states, and as liberalized regimes—some more democratic than others—have appeared in Asia and Latin America, the role of independent news media free from government control has been assumed, if not always carefully defined. Visits to some fifty countries in Eastern Europe, the former Soviet Union, East Asia and Latin America—all professing democracy, though varying widely in what that means and how it is best accomplished—provide evidence that democracy and freedom of the press have different meanings in countries that are redefining themselves.

In the three most visible countries of East Central Europe—Poland, the Czech Republic and Hungary—national nuances guide new media laws, the flowering and contraction of new media, what it means to be a journalist and what journalists write about civil society. Freedom of the press has sometimes meant the appearance of a new journalism infused with American ideas about separating fact from opinion, only to be followed by the return of a more interpretative European model. It has meant a limitation on foreign ownership in some places and a welcoming attitude about any and all foreign capital—and thus ownership and control—in others. It has meant that government may hold on to state television while allowing cable competitors to have their way with the market. And it has seen leaders with democratic instincts retaliate against media they think too critical or socially irresponsible.

Above all, the new freedom has meant experimentation with direct and indirect government by the people. Individual and institutional liberty has generally meant an embrace of market economies and capitalism, though this is not necessarily a requirement for democracy, some commentators would argue. In fact, in many countries, the movement from command to market economies has been slow, with the two systems existing concurrently and sometimes clashing with each other.

It is perhaps not startling that emerging democracies are not of one mind concerning the role and function of the news media. Even in the United States, after more than 200 years of experimentation, there is still little agreement about the role and rights of the media—save that the First Amendment, which commands no prior restraint of publication, is invoked by all as a basis for the freedom of the press. For some the First Amendment suggests an "anything goes" approach to free expression, with the only acceptable intervention being that of the courts, where citizens can bring suit for impairment to individual rights, such as privacy, reputation, property and the sanctity of one's home. But the American people are in considerable disagreement as to whether the media ought to promote a sense of community or widen conflicts through critical reporting and comment. There is agreement in theory that the free flow of information and opinions are the essential preconditions of press freedom, but, of course, these wide options can and do collide with individual rights, political and social policies, and private interests.

There is much talk about the press as an adversary of government or as a checking device in the Fourth Estate formulation. Still other commentators think that the news media are the central nervous system of society and ought to act responsibly and constructively to help the public better define and develop democracy. While the news media often reflect the bravado of the adversary label, truly critical, adversarial journalism, such as extensive investigative reporting, is more often the exception than the rule.

To be sure, the role of media in democracy cannot be taken for granted, whether in the highly developed democracies of the West or in more fragile new systems. In Argentina and Brazil newly democratic governments speak warmly of press freedom but urge harsh libel laws or suggest that unlicensed journalists be fined and jailed. In Malaysia and Singapore government leaders say press freedom is essential to democracy, but insist that the media help develop the society by preaching cooperation rather than criticism. In Russia journalists rightly fear for their lives as they attempt to make sense of their turbulent and fragmented society. In several countries, controls on ownership, journalistic practice, newsprint costs and state advertising "guide" the free media.

Even defining press freedom proves difficult for those who watch closely. Freedom House, a nonprofit study group, confidently divides the world's press into three categories—free, partly free and not free—understanding all the while that these labels will stimulate denials and disagreement.

The debate between freedom and responsibility and whether the media should be formally or informally accountable engages the media, the state and other institutions and individuals in scores of countries. In the United States absolutists on First Amendment rights say that there can be no qualification on freedom, that the Constitution makes no requirement that the press be responsible. This claim, while true, rings hollow in a society that has a complex system of media law and regulation and thousands of lawyers acting otherwise. The respected but rarely consulted Hutchins Commission on Freedom of the Press proposed a "representative picture" theory for the press, one that would allow the various "constituent groups" of society a fair place in the coverage and content of the media. Fifty years after that report was issued, this suggestion has largely been ignored. However, there have been efforts to make the work force more representative, which may or may not lead to some idealized representative content.

The U.S. media system (and the philosophy behind it) are greatly admired the world over, but that does not mean that any and all aspects of the First Amendment can be exported. That was one of the flaws in the well-intentioned efforts of American media, government and foundation leaders who developed assistance and training programs in independent Africa after 1960 and in the former communist world after 1989. While assistance was welcomed at first, the dogmatism of some true believers in the U.S. system was not. Legions of

American editors and broadcasters, as well as others from Western Europe, swarmed into countries from which they had previously been barred. Much of the boost offered was appreciated and led to the development of assertive local media and journalistic organizations, but at times the American approach was not always applicable since so much of journalistic practice must comport with local customs and culture. Ironically, some poorly informed Americans came armed with a "we won the Cold War" swagger, giving less than adequate credit to local journalists, some of whom suffered greatly through torture and jail to establish their new media.

If the link between media and government in the formulation of democracy is difficult to define, so is any understanding of the extent to which democratic values should prevail in journalistic content and in newsroom operations. Some journalists in the new democracies assumed that editors and station managers should be elected in democratic fashion, while expressing puzzlement about the rather autocratic nature of U.S. media management, which professes democracy for others but in the workplace typically chooses autocracy for itself. In the 1960s when a Burlington, Iowa daily, *The Hawk Eye,* had an election for managing editor, in the fashion of the French daily *Le Monde,* ridicule abounded in the trade press and at professional meetings. While employee ownership has occasionally been experimented with, it is clear that the structure of media in the United States must live in harmony with the market economy and commercialism, there being no viable democratic alternative at the moment.

In the opening section of this issue, "Definitive Questions," essays by Leo Bogart and Denis McQuail explore the contemporary relationship between media and democracy and its implications for the future. The next section, "Media and the Dynamics of Democracy Around the World," opens with Václav Havel and Boutros Boutros-Ghali, former secretary-general of the United Nations. They are joined by contributors who examine the relationship between media and democracy in specific locations around the world: Michael Schudson, Orville Schell, Sevanti Ninan, Joe Davidson, María Luisa MacKay, Adam Michnik, Gábor Demszky, Monroe E. Price, and John Maxwell Hamilton and George A. Krimsky.

"Journalism as a Democratic Discipline" explores the demands that democracy makes on journalists in essays by Robert MacNeil, Brian Mulroney, Victor Navasky, Davis Merritt, Donald W. Shriver Jr., Nancy

Hicks Maynard, Margaret T. Gordon, and Andie Tucher and Dan Bischoff. In our final selection of essays, "Democracy and New Media," Lawrence K. Grossman, Sara B. Ivry and Andrew C. Gordon consider the implications for democracy of new media technologies. Christopher Dornan concludes this issue with a review essay assaying recent books on media and democracy.

Generally, *democratic* media means media that support the democratic system of free elections, majority rule, political freedom, political equality, minority rights, representative government and an independent judiciary. And since freedom itself means a lack of restraint, it is assumed that media can operate unfettered at least until they collide with individual rights or institutional interests. Ideally, democracy and media coexist and support each other through a process of negotiation hopefully aimed at developing a consensus about the public interest.

Everette E. Dennis
Robert W. Snyder

I

Definitive Questions

1

Media and Democracy

Leo Bogart

Do mass media, inherently, serve democracy? Does the rapid evolution of ever more advanced communications technology foster the
dissemination and exchange of information and ideas in a tolerant
spirit? The fast and conventional answer to these two questions is yes.
The rise of democratic theory and practice is linked historically to the
invention of printing. The growth of literacy spread ideas that subverted and delegitimated the long-established authoritarian political
order and that widened the arena of public debate essential to representative government.

The worldwide diffusion of democratic ideals would seem to be a
necessary byproduct of mass communications. Just as anarchist and
socialist pamphlets smuggled from Western Europe once undermined
the czarist regime, Radio Liberty and the BBC nurtured opposition in
the Soviet Union. Fax messages encouraged the student demonstrators
at Tiananmen Square. Satellite broadcasting and the Internet have a
global reach that is difficult or impossible for repressive governments
to control. The forces that have been set in motion seem irresistible.
How can they fail to lead to the triumphant ascendancy of the democratic ideal?

A sober look at how media work in today's world suggests that they
remain vulnerable to manipulation—by political authorities motivated
by ideological zeal or crude self-interest, or by economic forces that
limit their resources, their variety and their integrity. They are not
inevitably an agent of democracy.

3

But democracy is hard to define. No single political system can lay exclusive claim to the term, and it is not at all certain that we know it when we see it. Democracy has been described as an ideal, often defined by what it opposes, rather than as an operational format for any specific kind of government. Certainly the contemporary variations on the democratic model all differ radically from its prototype in Periclean Athens, where the citizen minority of the population could be assembled for discussion and the voices of individual orators heard by all. But all democracies share certain important precepts—open debate, with sufferance of unpopular opinions, and decisions taken by honest voting and thereupon accepted.

The trappings and nomenclature of democracy are pervasive. Hence the adoption of the term, "people's democracies," by the dismal and brutal appendages of the Soviet empire; hence the expensive flummery of plebiscites and pseudo-elections in which even the most vicious dictatorships indulge. (Announcing a 91 percent turnout and a 95 percent vote for his reelection, Kazakhstan's President Nursultan Nazarbayev scoffs at Western critics: "We are Asian countries. We have our own certain mentality.")

The emergence of representative democratic government corresponded to the needs of a numerically enlarged and physically dispersed community. Representative democracy is inconceivable without forms of mass communication—to create awareness of public issues that face a society whose members are not personally in touch with each other, who lack common geographic reference points, and whose central institutions are remote from the people they serve or exploit.

Democracy is usually thought of as a product of Western Enlightenment thinking, but many of the critical questions that revolve around the linkage of media and democracy occur in the nonindustrial world. The strength and sophistication of national mass communications systems reflect the overall state of economic and technological development. In wealthy, literate and democratic countries, patterns of media consumption and political participation differ enormously for various incomes and social classes. These patterns reflect the cost of individual media as consumer goods, the complexity of the information they deliver and the amount of time and effort required for their use.

Even in open societies, the barriers of poverty and illiteracy can fragment national media experiences. In most poor countries, the mass that forages for subsistence coexists with an elite whose members enjoy many of the perquisites of the good life in the West, including ready access to information. India and Brazil observe democratic practices like free elections and free expression. Their media institutions are highly developed, but accessibility to various elements of the population is heavily imbalanced. Any answer to the question of whether media serve democracy must be qualified: which media, and among what parts of the public?

Even an authoritarian government may tolerate some independent media expressions. In Tunisia, for example, books forbidden in Arabic (which might stimulate dangerous thoughts among the masses) may be published in French (where they will be read only by the elite). Nonetheless, newspapers cannot be imported from France because their content is most likely to hit close to home.

The present regimes of Serbia and Croatia tolerate one free news service, as well as opposition newspapers and radio stations, but find ways to throttle their advertising. Independent newspapers pay a triple price for newsprint, so the opposition Belgrade paper, *Nasa Borba,* even with a gift of newsprint from the European Commission, costs readers three times as much as the regime's own *Borba.* Serb President Slobodan Milosevic meets daily with the head of Belgrade Radio-Television, presumably not to review the Nielsen overnight program ratings.

Today, no national media system can be hermetically sealed off. Satellite dishes can be outlawed, articles in imported news magazines can be selectively clipped and photographs blacked out, foreign films can be banned or cut, and wire services censored. Still, somehow or other, the word gets through. Though not entirely. For instance, news of the American moon landing was suppressed in China. I recently asked a leading Chinese journalist how and when the news had finally gotten out. The answer: "Oh, did the Americans land on the moon? I thought it was the Russians."

Media power is political power. At dawn on October 1, 1991, a small band of soldiers took over Radio Lomé in Togo. Putting a pistol to the head of a newscaster, they forced him to broadcast a communiqué announcing the end of the civilian government. "Military music and cries to the glory of President Gnassingbe Eyadema rounded out the program," according to a Panos Institute report. In the same year, the rebels who sought to topple Russia's new democratic government took the Ostankino television station as one of their principal targets. Years earlier, when the Bolsheviks had moved quickly to take over complete control of the press, they cynically proclaimed their doctrine that it should be an instrument of the party's purposes. Lenin denounced the abolition of censorship. "In reality," he said, "this is not freedom of the press, but freedom to deceive the oppressed and exploited masses of the people by the rich, the bourgeoisie." Years afterwards, a large neon sign in Moscow read, "The Soviet Press—Strongest Weapon of Leninist Power."

The function of the media, according to totalitarian doctrine, was to guide the masses. Germany's press, radio and film industries were as advanced as any in the world, both in technology and in quality of content, when the Nazis took over. By the time the owners of the *Frankfurter Zeitung* "presented" their once-respected newspaper to Adolph Hitler as a birthday present, it was already an instrument of Goebbels' comprehensive propaganda machine.

Cunning advocates of tyranny can use the media to threaten freedom. The Ayatollah Khomeini, who came to power with the help of audiocassette sermons smuggled into Iran, displayed the ultimate act of intolerance when he imposed a death sentence *in absentia* upon the novelist Salman Rushdie. Throughout the Middle East, the Islamic equivalents of American TV evangelists are a dominant presence on state-run radio and television—tolerated and feared by the regimes in power. Their familiar bearded faces adorn the covers of fundamentalist tracts that preach hatred for what, in the West, would be considered civil society.

The overt censorship that cruder dictatorships practice is today a less common form of inhibiting free political expression than media conformity to fit official expectations. A multiplicity of media channels would seem to raise the likelihood that deviant opinions or unwanted facts might break through to public awareness. However, any lone, off-key voice within a large chorus is unlikely to find many listeners. If it becomes obtrusive and offensive to the powers that be, it can quickly be contained and sealed off. Today's Lebanon, still torn by partisan divisions, has some 40 television channels serving a population of 3.5 million. This may create the illusion of diversity, but all alike are restrained by knowing what is acceptable to the Syrian occupation forces. The sheer number of media voices is not a good indicator of a society's level of freedom.

[Authoritarian nations are not the only ones in which political power and media power go together. In some democratic countries, media ownership has reached what many would consider to be dangerous levels of concentration.]At this writing, in the United Kingdom, Rupert Murdoch's News Corporation has 37 percent of the daily national newspaper circulation; dailies owned by Robert Hersant, who was imprisoned for his wartime collaboration with the Nazis, account for over a third of the national circulation in France, and for two-fifths in Poland; [in Italy, Silvio Berlusconi owns the top three commercial television channels and three pay-TV channels along with newspapers and magazines. All forcefully backed his political party. When he became prime minister, he placed his confederates in four out of the five directorships of state broadcasting.]

Links between those who wield political power and those who own the organs of mass communication may be inescapable, but they are nonetheless disquieting. The American media system, while it sustains a hugely variegated array of expressions, has become steadily more concentrated in its control by a handful of large corporations, themselves increasingly linked in joint ventures, many of them designed to explore new forms of communication.

"The public leads and we follow," says the marketing and advertising director of the world's largest advertiser, Procter & Gamble. But the public leads only through the maze of choices that Procter & Gamble and its giant contemporaries have already laid out. Since the public's taste is largely formed by the existing television programming structure, shows that provoke political reflection generally meet with blind indifference. However, advertising introduces a dazzling and constantly changing array of fresh images into everyday life—thus ever raising aspirations and challenging the status quo. In this respect, it fosters democracy.

The rich diversity of media in the advanced industrial countries is impossible to separate from their enormous advertising base. [The companies that provide the advertising revenues that now sustain most mass media have a stake in the established economic and political order.] Their interests are likely to be challenged only at the (nonadvertising-dependent) fringes of the media system.] The resulting conservatism and self-censorship, longstanding targets of Marxist criticism, defy the proposition that media inherently serve democracy.)

[Is a market-controlled media system essential to serve the democratic process? Media choices require an economic underpinning. A media market can only exist in a thriving economy.)

It is hard to imagine a rigidly controlled state economy that would tolerate the kind of political challenge that an independent press represents. However, one need not equate a non-market economy with mobs of identically clad thousands, chanting and waving little red books. Sweden and Israel, nations with a strong socialist component in their economies, have coexisted with a free press. The example of the BBC can always be trotted out to demonstrate that, with the right safeguards, professional journalism can maintain its autonomy within the confines of what remains essentially a government institution. But the BBC's inability to satisfy the public's desire for choices illustrates the virtues of the market, if not its utter necessity.

If market forces can both expand and diminish the democratic possibilities of the media, the same can be said for the professional norms and practices of journalists. The media surely cannot be blamed if U.S. voting rates are low, if there is massive collective amnesia for the names of prominent public officials, appallingly vague memory for geography, and utter confusion or apathy over much-debated public issues. However, the media have evidently failed to compensate for the deficiencies of our national character and our educational system.

Mass media can support democracy only through information and ideas, but the bulk of mass media content—especially in audiovisual media—is dedicated to entertainment. This cannot be categorized as nonpolitical. It is *anti*-political, because it deflects public time and attention away from real-world matters that invariably carry political connotations.

While visual images may convey experiences and evoke empathy more vividly than words, printed text is unsurpassed in its ability to arouse indignation and to stir the reflection and deliberation that are essential to the democratic process. The steady decline of newspaper competition in the United States, and the (partly resultant) attrition in newspaper readership, have meant diminished exposure to the clash of ideas, to differing viewpoints about local events. This has serious consequences for citizens' interest in government, since local television and radio news, preoccupied with recitations of innumerable minor crimes and disasters, hardly ever address real civic issues.

Media operating by the rules of the market subordinate the deadly realities of journalism to fill idle hours with the transient amusements of the lurid and the trivial. In 1927, long before Court TV, eight-second sound bites and daytime TV magazine shows, Walter Lippmann pondered the sensationalism of the press and wrote:

> We do not, for example, know how to imagine what the consequences will be of attempting to conduct popular government with an electorate which is subjected to a series of disconnected, but all in their moments absolutely absorbing, hullabaloos. . . . It means the turning away of popular interest from a continuing interest in public affairs. . . . I am inclined to ask myself whether in view of the technical complexity of almost all great public questions, it is really possible any longer for the mass of voters to form significant public opinions. . . . The usual rhetoric of politics has in the meantime gone stale, and it cannot begin to compete in vividness and human interest with the big spectacles of murder, love, death, and triumphant adventure which the new publicity is organized to supply. The management of affairs tends, therefore, once again to rest in a governing class, a class which is not hereditary, which is without titles, but is none the less obeyed and followed.

The rise of today's so-called "media elite" became an issue in the 1992 election campaign; it will surface again.

The media system is steadily more international in scope and control, with influence flowing overwhelmingly from west to east (or from north to south, in today's preferred jargon). This tendency is fed by the inexhaustible audience demand for greater choice, which has forced state broadcasting authorities to open up more channels and state broadcasting monopolies to give way to private owners. This may, in a very small way, facilitate the spread of democratic values at the same time that it expedites the attrition of indigenous national cultures.

Imported entertainment carries a political message, insofar as it represents exposure to different values, modes of behavior and living standards. Its most disruptive elements arise in its depiction of human relationships, especially those between men and women. In nonindustrial countries, resistance to foreign films and television programs generally takes the form of moralizing objections to their prurient aspects, but these complaints mask a discomfort with the deeper and more disturbing forces that they set in motion.

[Unlike the charades of fiction, news constantly reinforces the connections between each individual and the surrounding society.][Americans used to read the newspaper to help them form their opinions. Now newspapers and television tell them what their opinions are.] Pre-election polls and other opinion surveys have evolved in this century in step with the parallel and unrelated evolution of social science and product marketing. Their emergence as a leading ingredient of the news raises new questions about the relationship of the media to democracy.

Surveys have surely sensitized everyone in political life to shifts in the popular temper and public awareness of significant issues. But polls have had a pernicious effect on political candidates who follow the precepts of market research rather than their own considered and conscientiously arrived-at policy choices. Media have made polls a subject of frivolous entertainment, changing coverage of election campaigns away from reports on principled debate to tracking who's ahead.

The lead stories of leading newspapers and network newscasts are often dedicated to the meaningless answers given to simplistic questions on complex subjects. ("Are you for or against a balanced budget amendment?" is a recent prototype of this nonsense, which bypasses such fundamental issues as what a Constitution is for, and how the budget is to be balanced without sacrifices that no one seems willing to make.) The answers to such nonquestions are in turn invoked by politicians to support their already fixed positions.

The ultimate expression of this phenomenon is the idea of government by instant polling, as advocated by Ross Perot during the course of the 1994 presidential race. Snap judgments influenced by question-wording, with responses from an unrepresentative self-appointed minority of the electorate, would become a substitute for the reflection and debate that properly precede any legislative or executive decision in a democratic political order.

Polling is only one element in the complex array of influences that media bring to bear on public policy formation in a society with an insatiable thirst for amusement. Will the balance of entertainment and information tilt once again? Electronic data services hold out the promise of encyclopedic knowledge resources within reach of a new generation of computer-literate Americans. The Internet has grown at an exponential rate. Its devotees speak of the rise of a new sense of community as computer-linked interest groups form and multiply, their members sharing intimate thoughts and evolving emotional ties. They believe that the Internet, with its open access to any form of specialized knowledge, represents a new form of egalitarian democracy. Against the optimistic vision of humanity linked by the Web, however, may be set the more compelling scenario of a nation ever more

sharply divided into information haves and have-n⟨
gap widened by the disparity in mastery of technol
knowledge.

And new media can be used to undermine a ⟨
well as to enhance it. The terrorists who bombed the federⁱⁱ.
in Oklahoma City in 1995 were part of a network that uses advanceu
communications technologies to disseminate messages of violence and
hate. Some 250 neo-Nazi groups are linked through shortwave radio,
fax, the Internet, computer bulletin boards, desktop publishing and
public access television.

⟨Media are instruments.⟩They can serve different ends. They are
indispensable to a democratic society because they make information
available at all social levels and in all its geographic corners. They are
essential as critics of government, as investigators of wrongdoing, as
advocates of good (as well as not-so-good) causes.⟨They are a forum
for discussion and debate. They create and define the separate con-
stituencies whose compromises make democracy work. At the same
time, by creating common experiences, offering shared symbols and
giving the public a sense of contact with its leaders, they offer a
constant reminder of national identity.

⟨However, the existence of an advanced and diverse media system
does not guarantee that it will serve democracy. Monolithic control
over mass communications is no longer possible, but control need not
be total to be effective. Mass media can serve democracy only when
those who manage them feel a passionate responsibility to create it
and maintain it. ⟩ ✓good much used

---

*Leo Bogart, a 1989–90 Media Studies Center senior fellow and former
executive vice president and general manager of the Newspaper Advertising Bureau, is the author* of Commercial Culture: The Media
System and the Public Interest *and* Cool Words, Cold War.

2

New Roles for New Times?

Denis McQuail

It is widely suspected that fundamental changes are undermining the traditional roles of the media in democracy. These roles are embedded both in the largely unwritten understandings of professional journalism and also in the expectations of politicians and citizen-audiences. For most of this century, especially in Western democracies, it has been largely up to the press to ensure that voters are well informed and capable of actively participating in public life, to subject politicians and governments to scrutiny and evaluation, and to express public feeling and provide a platform for ideas.

By and large, such expectations have been fulfilled. There are growing doubts, however, about the future. The media are entering a new phase of potentially fundamental change driven by technological and market forces. New technology increases the individualization and privatization of media use. In a postmodern consumerist society, the media and their content are more and more depoliticized and "secularized." Enhanced competitive pressures for audiences and advertisers in the media marketplace are such that commercial criteria take precedence over other values. The widespread rise of "tabloid television," infotainment and old-fashioned sensationalism are symptomatic of deeper changes. To compound the problem, this marketplace is increasingly global and the media are becoming detached from their local and national roots, where politics properly belong.

There are divided views about how far new media are bringing with them solutions to these problems. They have a liberating and democratizing potential, but they are also subject to the same pressures of commodification and privatization as the traditional media. The most innovative developments in communication technologies are those which, initially at least, serve a privileged minority rather than the mass of people. Developments are not, in any case, promoted because they advance democracy, but according to their economic potential. The new communication networks which are developing often cross-cut the older boundaries of place, culture, class and political organization and tend to undermine rather than sustain traditional political ties. Their general tendency is socially fragmenting rather than cohesive.

The implications for democratic politics are indeed worrying. There appears to be a decline in all things public, and democratic politics are nothing if not public and collective. The sphere or space for public debate is narrowed and fewer people actually participate as citizens and voters. Public opinion, the classic ingredient of democracy, is weakened and diluted. It is less rooted in information and belief, more trivial in the range of topics it refers to, and less widely shared by identifiable political communities. It may also be judged less autonomous and less easy to accept as expressing the state of mind of a citizen body. The media, which classically led and expressed public opinion, have increasingly lent themselves as tools for the manipulation of states of mind and the fabrication of supposed realities.

From the standpoint of a somewhat idealized notion of the democratic role of the media, the outlook is gloomy. Even so, more positive interpretations are viable. The capacity of the media to store, process, access and distribute large volumes of information at steadily declining costs is rapidly expanding. Certain individuals and groups may well have a greater potential for informed engagement with political issues. It is more difficult for authorities to monopolize information and to control access. Spatial barriers to the flow of information and ideas can no longer be defended. Some of the historic world changes of our times, such as the decline or fall of communism and the end of apartheid have plausibly been attributed to the communication revolution as much as to political revolution.

Whether one is a pessimist or an optimist, there is little doubt that things are changing fundamentally, and a reassessment of the media-politics relationship is high on the agenda for those who care about democracy. Politicians and political parties, whether in or out of office, are often the first to voice anxieties and frustrations about the role of the mass media. They feel much less in charge. They can no longer set the terms of access, even to their own potential supporters. They have to submit to the requirements of the media, both as to what topics deserve attention and the manner of their presentation. Increasingly, the second of these determines the first, making politics more lively and entertaining but also more superficial and irrelevant.

Relevance is judged more by the media's assessment of the average audience attention span than by any considered view of the interests of society. At the same time, the media concentrate on personalities and search for scandal, venality and wrongdoing. Such tendencies, taken together, do little to enrich the public discourse and tend to weaken the attachment of citizens to their political leaders. They work against a mature political culture, which requires information, engagement and some measure of trust and altruism.

Reviewing the situation in this way, it is clear that much more is involved than media change alone. Politics is also changing. It is less based on coherent and competing belief systems. It is more pragmatic than ever before. It has often become fragmented into causes and issues which have little coherent interconnection. It is arguably more manipulative and even cynical. Democratic political institutions have found it difficult to change, partly because they have a "sacred" character, but also because of numerous vested interests in old forms and rituals.

This fossilization also applies to the political role of the media. The traditional relationship between politics and the newspaper press rested on several historical circumstances, with variations from country to country. In general, newspapers often had links with particular political parties or standpoints, whether these links stemmed from an identification with a certain place or readership, or with particular organizations. News was, above all, an account of political or economic events. The press gave privileged access to those with political power, especially governments, national or local. It typically claimed to serve some notion, however partisan, of the national or community interest.

To a large extent, the readerships of newspapers coincided, whether for reasons of media organization, geography or social composition, with current political groupings. The newspaper could be trusted or distrusted by readers, counted on or discounted by politicians, according to a familiar and dependable decoding scheme. This condition of intimate press-politics relations, however, is rapidly disintegrating as a result of current media and social changes.

This diagnosis points to a more fundamental parting of the ways between politics and the media. Ever since television was recognized as a political influence to be reckoned with, it has been at the receiving end of two opposing forces. On the one hand, broadcasting was defined as a new democratic force capable of uniting communities and nations, over and above the divisions and self-interests of party politics. It had an evident potential to contribute to informed, rational and shared civic experience. From time to time and here and there, this potential has been realized.

On the other hand, television has been subject to a variety of efforts to bend it to the dominant political will or, failing that, to neutralize it as a factor. The publicity industries foster in politics recurring dreams of television-led popularity. But the predominant stance of politicians towards television (certainly when in office) has been one of fear of the uncertainties, risks and failures inherent in television appearances. Complicating the situation has been the increased pressure to maximize the economic return from television as a business, a pressure that has reached a point where discussions of the ideal political role of television have become academic—literally as well as figuratively.

Despite the promise of a new age of democratic political communication made possible by broadcast television, it looks as if a combination of commercialism and the over-caution of politicians has denied its realization. Perceived as potent and unpredictable, television has been held at arm's length from politics. We see this in the too-careful allocation of time between major contenders for office in many countries, the taboos attached to editorializing, the suspicion of debates and of the presence of cameras in forums of debate and the limited access to views which deviate far from dominant consensus. Politicians dislike the fact that a new elite of television anchors, interviewers and personalities has come to control access to the public.

The divergence of interests between the media and institutionalized politics manifests itself in a number of different ways. The audiences now mainly sought and valued by television are not, on the whole, the ones valued by politicians. They are less likely to be truly mass audiences and they are not very disposed to listen to political messages. The relevant parameters of audience composition conform to media marketing and advertising criteria rather than social or political background and motivations. Whatever else, "mainstream" television does not seem to fulfill its potential to widen and deepen public attention to matters of political debate.

When we think of television as a means of political communication we are now more likely to think of it as a means of political marketing and would-be manipulation rather than as a valued participant in the democratic process. Politicians are groomed for television, information is selectively fed to television, broadcasters are courted or flattered (and occasionally bullied). Campaign activities are coordinated to fit television schedules. Yet the belief that television would dominate politics has proved to be a half-truth, at best. It takes an undue prominence in the thinking of politicians, it is evidently important to citizens as a source of impressions and guide to events, but it has little power of its own and it generally plays a very limited and subordinate role in the political process.

We are thus entering an age of new interactive communication technology at a time when relations between politics and media are strained and unsatisfactory. In Western Europe generally, the continued vitality of public broadcasting institutions has helped to stave off any crisis, but the strains are evident. For somewhat different reasons, the same broad diagnosis applies to the newly established liberal democratic systems in Eastern Europe and the former Soviet Union. In general, political uses of the media were suspect because of the long dominance by one party and by the state. In the post-communist environment and climate, there are still hopes that television, along with the press, will play an important role in re-establishing a more open and honest political life. This expectation has been partially fulfilled, but citizens still tend to be suspicious of political involvements on the part of the media, and commercial forces are undermining trust from another direction. The political role of the media remains very uncertain.

Journalism cannot make up for the deficiencies of politics, but it remains an indispensable ingredient in the democratic process. What the media choose to do or not do is going to matter to the quality of democratic life. Current electronic media innovations are unlikely to fundamentally alter the *public* character of most media experience. Despite diversification and specialization, the *mass* media are not disappearing and most national societies are characterized by shared political concerns. If nothing else, the O.J. Simpson media mania has confirmed the power of a presumed mass interest.

But a new division of labor is emerging, as political functions of media are dispersed across a growing spectrum of media types, channels and networks. Currently the tasks of political communication are shared across the media more or less as follows: Print media provide fuller accounts of events, act as critics and help to anchor political beliefs and party commitments. Television and radio are showcases for personalities and vehicles for planned publicity. They also provide a window for spectatorship and observation on selected kinds of political events.

It is still unclear where the new electronic media will fit into this picture. They are only just beginning to operate as sources of specialized information and networking in relation to special issues. But the new media still only serve actively involved minorities and do little for the cohesion or participation of the many. They also seem to be developing according to an apolitical model, with little expectation that they will serve collective ends. They are essentially individualistic in use and utilitarian or hedonistic in their bias. Despite their relative freedom, they have not yet been acclaimed for any rejuvenating effects on politics.

There is clearly a rich potential in the variety and abundance of media now available, but it is hard to identify new and vital forms and applications with respect to political communication. While one can make a case that proliferating TV and radio talk shows and other audience-participatory formats are reconnecting politics with everyday life and ordinary people, the driving spirit of these communication events seems deeply apolitical in the traditional meaning of the term.

Political communication is in a problematic condition, for which there may be no solution. Some may pin their faith on hypothetical claims about new media as more participant, interactive and democratic than "old media." They may also envisage as yet untried forms of plebiscitary "teledemocracy." But if one is confident about neither of these prospects, it makes sense to draw on traditional notions of the role of the media in a healthy democratic political culture.

From this perspective, the following elements continue to matter most: First, mass media will still be needed to define and publicize the shared issues, objectives or problems of the society and of the wider international community. Secondly, there will need to be widely available expressions of alternative beliefs, opinions and value commitments which relate to these issues. Thirdly, sources of information, ideas and comment which can be perceived as *trustworthy* will remain indispensable, especially in an age of over-abundant information. Necessary conditions of media trustworthiness are independence, openness about value commitments and transparency of ownership and control. Fourth, broad opportunities for access to public channels of communication, including old and new media, will need to be maintained, for collective as well as for individual voices.

Of course, there is something very familiar about the roles implied in these priorities. They reassert the expectations that media should help set public policy agendas, express diverse opinions and beliefs, reinforce allegiances and act as critics of powerful institutions. They presuppose a value to reside both in social conflict as well as in cooperation as conditions for social progress. They presume continued need (and demand) for journalistic professionalism and editorial autonomy. They derive support from values of socially responsible reporting. They indicate support for public broadcasting as an independent and alternative component in a predominantly commercial media environment.

This is not a call for a more politically committed press which tries unilaterally to make good the deficiencies of politics or to compensate for the secularizing trends of our age. The partisan press model cannot be artificially resurrected, any more than the state-controlled model can be reintroduced in Eastern Europe. But there is also nothing wrong with partisanship, advocacy and committed journalism as components in a diverse system. Their contemporary absence may have more to do with industrialization and commercialization of media than with their declining relevance. In considering the democratic requirements from media, we do not need to differentiate among the essential needs of mature, newer or re-established democracies, even if local conditions will continue to vary a good deal. The convergence of media technologies will not have ironed out deep cultural differences, and economic differences will persist. Finally, we need political journalism which is popular and accessible without loss of integrity or information quality.

It is unlikely that the desirable goals outlined can be attained (or maintained) without conscious efforts by "society" and thus not by market and technological forces on their own. "Society" is not an abstraction, but stands for concrete and organized efforts by those who care about the health of democracy. This also implies the existence of a public interest in mass media which is more than the sum of individual "user" demands. The whole idea may sound a little old-fashioned (it is certainly not new), but there is no logical reason why the technological changes under way should have made it obsolescent. It is also just as valid in a more competitive, globalized and commercialized age as it ever was.

Denis McQuail, a 1988–89 Media Studies Center senior fellow, is professor and former chairman of the Department of Mass Communication at the University of Amsterdam in the Netherlands. He is also an editor of the European Journal of Communication *and joint director of the Netherlands Press Foundation.*

II

Media and the Dynamics of Democracy Around the World

3

Opinion—The New Authority

Boutros Boutros-Ghali

Democracy is perhaps the most ancient form of government, finding its roots in clans and tribes before the age of dictators. Over the centuries democracy came to be seen as a ideal. But all too often it was a fragile plant in those lands where it was allowed to grow. Without question its finest flowering has been, as in Tocqueville's title, *Democracy in America.* In the course of establishing democracy in this country, challenge after challenge to it has been faced, from within and without.

What is new about democracy today? It no longer is an ideal for many but a reality for only a few. Peoples and governments in every part of the globe now are striving to establish the institutions and foster the mentalities which democracy needs in order to flourish. The peoples who now clamor for democratic life are aware that every aspect of human betterment today—social, political, security, environmental and economic—cannot long endure unless guaranteed by democratic processes.

The media are the second new factor. Thomas Jefferson famously declared that he would prefer newspapers without government to a government without newspapers. Jefferson's advice may still be correct, but the power and prestige of what we call "the media" have outstripped our ability to fully understand this phenomenon. The media today are as important as the branches of government, and have a direct impact on each of them: the executive, the legislature and even the judiciary.

Of even greater significance is the media's impact on democracy itself. The media convey information directly to individuals. The media conduct opinion polls, which appear to have "scientific" validity. The media take editorial positions based on public opinion.

This process is transforming democracy. For the past two centuries, it was *law* that provided the source of authority for democracy. Today, law seems to be replaced by *opinion* as the source of authority, and the media serve as the arbiters of public opinion. The implications of this transformation are vast, but we as yet do not clearly understand them.

What we do know is that the media in all their forms—print, image and electronic impulse—must be free. I was once a journalist and I know that freedom of the media can be denied in many ways. Presses can be smashed. Journalists can be kidnapped or shot. But there are other insidious ways to effectively curb the freedom of the press.

As we consider together the new phenomenon of the media, let us declare as our number one principle: The press must be free. I assure you that I will do all I can as secretary-general to see that the United Nations upholds the words of Article 19 of the Universal Declaration of Human Rights: "Everyone has the right. . .to seek, receive and impart information and ideas through any media regardless of frontiers."

Other principles also deserve attention and respect, even if they cannot be perfectly achieved. These are principles of scale, of time and of thought given to serious topics.

Universality of coverage is an important objective. Press attention is like a beam of light which illuminates where it shines but leaves all else in obscurity. In Angola, where a U.N. Mission is working for national reconciliation, more people have died than in all other current U.N. operations around the world put together. But the public knows very little of Angola.

Comprehensive coverage is also worth striving for. This may mean going back to report on a story when the main excitement is over. El Salvador was given space when the war was raging, but not much has been reported on the remarkable achievements since then. The aftermath of a story is rarely as captivating as the fast-breaking developments at the start. But the long-term consequences may be more significant, for far more people.

Intellectual coverage is also of value. I do not mean that a newspaper should try to resemble an academic journal, but ideas can often be more important than actions. Events dominate our lives, but trends of thought may be far more significant in shaping the future. This is a time in history when ideas are greatly in demand. The *Agenda for*

Peace and *Agenda for Development* that I have put forth are intended as contributions to the contest of ideas about peace, development and democracy. The debate is a legitimate and important topic for media attention.

Obviously, the principles I have mentioned here are those which the United Nations cares deeply about. The United Nations must by definition be universal. The United Nations must always try to stay the course until a long-term mission is complete. And the United Nations must both reflect and generate ideas—with the aim of establishing norms and standards for international progress.

The third new factor of our time is the United Nations itself. The United Nations created in San Francisco 50 years ago was not permitted to function as designed. The United Nations that in the Cold War shaped roles for itself in de-colonization, development assistance and peace keeping merits praise but cannot successfully continue without adapting to change.

A new United Nations is being constructed on the most compelling cases as they arise. There have been setbacks. There also have been successes. The successes have been hard-won, but are more likely to endure for just that reason.

A new structure for global stability and peace must be built. A new rationale and action plan for social development must be achieved. International law must be revitalized. Human rights—including the right of free expression in all forums—must be reaffirmed and defended.

In this noble effort there is no turning back for the United Nations. A crucial recognition is now required. We are all in this together. The United Nations is not simply a mechanism for the use of its member states. It provides a forum for ideas. It provides a voice for the most deprived. It provides a system for international peace and security. It provides a continuum of conferences to address new global issues. It provides legitimacy for international action. It rests on the great achievements of the past, and it is in the forefront of creating new foundations for the future.

Boutros Boutros-Ghali was secretary-general of the United Nations from 1992 until 1996. He was Egypt's minister of state for foreign affairs from October 1977 until May 1991. His essay is adapted from his keynote address at the Media Studies Center's 10th anniversary conference in 1995.

4

A Soul of the Soul

Václav Havel

It is said that the press is a seventh superpower. I don't know which superpower it is, but it is definitely a superpower. It carries a great deal of responsibility for our common fate, for what we come to know and what we don't, what we should worry about and what we shouldn't, what we should believe in and what we should not. In its own way, the press—as a part of the information and communication system of today's civilization—is a soul of the soul of all mankind. It is a medium of self-understanding.

I certainly don't need to emphasize too much why I am saying all this. I'm saying it to underline the importance of the press, the importance of its freedom, cultural standards, intelligence and responsibility.

In closing, allow me one personal note: after decades of oppression, Czechoslovakia also has an absolutely free press. A great number of various newspapers of the most diverse kind and focus are published here. All dailies that are to appear on the newsstands in the morning come to my apartment around 11 p.m. the night before. I anxiously await the moment and immediately after I receive them, I start nervously leafing through them. Those are disquieting and often depressing moments. I find out how many new affairs and scandals broke out which will be later denied by someone during the day, how much unqualified, mean and often even rancorous critique was produced, how many various slanted interpretations of the same event and unjust mutual attacks tomorrow's papers will bring, and in reverse, how many important things they will irretrievably miss. So, about half an hour of my morning paper reading is taken by nervousness, anger and depression. But after about half an hour, when I digest all the nonsense that the papers print, I continue leafing through them, and I discover that I also find many interesting items of information, perception and analysis, each of them teaching me something and enriching me in some way. And a feeling of satisfaction and joy starts slowly but inexorably to push out my depression. And I go to bed almost euphoric because we are a free country and have a free press that activates the enormous creative potential which was until recently oppressed and kept in secret.

And always, long before falling asleep, I remember the wise words of an American judge who said—when he tried a newspaper for some disgusting slanders—"all the idiotic nonsense that all American newspapers write is a small, necessary and basically unimportant levy we pay for that immense, beautiful and vitally important gift that is the freedom of speech."

Allow me to close with a line from one of my unhappy characters in one of my allegedly absurd plays: "Long live freedom of speech!"

Václav Havel, playwright and president of the Czech Republic, delivered these remarks in 1992. They were translated by Suzanna Halsey.

5

Creating Public Knowledge

Michael Schudson

"No substantial famine," observes Amartya Sen, an economist who writes extensively about famines, "has ever occurred in a country with a democratic form of government and a relatively free press." This is an extraordinary remark. And Sen adds that this is so even for poor democracies beset by crop failures. Electoral democracy, with the support of the news media, prevents famines. When the audience for news is expanded, the shape of politics changes.

In a political democracy, the media are a vital force in keeping the concerns of the many in the field of vision of the governing few. News on television, radio, or in print, produced by journalists, is different from messages that a government official or corporate executive might deliver straight to the public on the Internet or by a direct mail circular. The difference is not only that the journalist has the opportunity, indeed the professional obligation, to frame the message. It is also that the newspaper story or television broadcast transforms an event or statement into the cultural form called news. A news story is an announcement of special interest and importance. It is a declaration by a familiar private (or sometimes public) and usually professional (but occasionally political) entity in a public place that an event is noteworthy. It suggests that what is published has a call on public attention. Placement on the page or in the broadcast indicates how noteworthy; readers and viewers understand the hierarchy or importance this creates. It is a hierarchy of moral salience. It is no wonder that the sacred center of the working day on a metropolitan newspaper is the editorial conference to decide what stories will make page one, and where on the page they will go.

The news gains power not in its direct impact on audiences but in the belief, justified in viable democracies, that the knowledge of citizens can from time to time be effective. The power of the press grows in a political culture characterized by this belief.

This is not to suggest that democracy needs no more than well distributed information. Information is not enough. But what can a citizenry do if it does have information? What would happen if professional journalists were free to provide the best information they could, undistorted by competitive feeding frenzies that center on matters irrelevant to the public good, unaffected by commercial requirements that displace political news for advertising, sports and recipes, uncensored by the fear that writing in depth about real politics will bore the public and doom the stories to go unread? If journalists could write what they wanted according to the highest ideals of the press, would democracy be saved?

To ask the questions is to recognize the answer: of course not. A public with information available to it is not an informed public. Even a public with information in its head is not necessarily a public with the motivation or frame of reference or capacity to act in a democracy. There is a difference between the "informational citizen," saturated with bits and bytes of information, and the informed citizen, the person who has not only information but a point of view and preferences with which to make sense of it.

The press cannot by itself create informed citizens, but can it do better than it has in serving democracy?

Better at exactly what? we might ask. I can imagine at least seven not altogether compatible goals a media system dedicated to democracy might aspire to:

1. The news media should provide citizens fair and full information so that they can make sound decisions as citizens. (In other words, the media should do just what most journalists say they try to do—with the unhappy effect, according to some critics, of boring or confusing people, and turning them away from politics.)
2. The news media should provide coherent frameworks to help citizens comprehend the complex political universe. They should analyze and interpret politics in ways that enable citizens to understand and to act.

(In other words, the media should do exactly what the professional goal of objectivity swears they should not do: interpret the news.)

3. The media should serve as common carriers of the perspectives of the varied groups in society; they should be, in the words of Herbert Gans, "multiperspectival." (In other words, the media should not provide an overarching coherence to the news, exactly the contrary of goal 2.)

4. The news media should provide the quantity and quality of news that people want; that is, the market should be the criterion for the production of news. (In other words, the news media should adhere to the rule that many critics insist drives the press toward the sensational, the prurient and the trivial.)

5. The media should represent the public and speak for and to the public interest in order to hold government accountable.

6. The news media should evoke empathy and provide deep understanding so that citizens at large can appreciate the situation of other human beings in the world and so elites can come to know and understand the situation of other human beings, notably nonelites, and learn compassion for them. (In other words, the news media should do exactly what diplomats who distrust compassion as a basis for foreign policy have roundly criticized them for doing in displaying the human plight of the people of Sarajevo and Somalia.)

7. The news media should provide a forum for dialogue among citizens that not only informs democratic decision making but is, as a process, an element in it.

The news media collectively do all these things today. In fact, a single news institution may attempt all seven impossible things before breakfast. But note that one objective may contradict the rest. And note as well that providing fair and accurate information, the measure by which the press is most often judged, is only one of many goals the press may hold out for itself. We are a long way from a coherent normative theory of journalism. And there is little to push news institutions to change this. Unlike the automobile industry or microelectronics, American journalism is not challenged from abroad. Unlike higher education, it is not stimulated by a diversity of models of excellence within. Diversity is not much admired inside journalism. The underground press, the partisan press, the alternative papers exist but are generally ignored. News stories trickle down from elite outlets to others, but the "trickle up" of significant stories is rare enough to excite comment or even a Pulitzer Prize. Journalism seems to ignore or denigrate what could be its most valuable seeds of change. Small may be beautiful in Amish quiltmaking or in the start-up of software companies, but not in journalism. Journalism, even at its research centers and with its foundation supporters, seems overcome with the charms of celebrity, commercial success, and national reach.

Although in other spheres, from medicine to welfare to social work to education, a focus on the formulation of public policy sharpens thought, most policy concerns in the news are entirely libertarian— just keep the government out. It is easy to have sympathy with that. But what follows is that the media do not have to think about themselves the way most other institutions do—as subject to public review and regulative public policies. Journalists' reflections on their own business are not tested in the discipline of actually having to influence institutional policy. In contrast, even a rube academic, working out the freshman general education course or revising admissions requirements, has more firsthand experience in policymaking than many experienced journalists who write about it.

The American news media may be the best in the world —although I doubt that political systems and cultures are comparable enough to make that a meaningful statement. American journalism may be better today than ever before—I believe this is so. But whether it serves democracy as well as it might is another matter, about which the press speaks in pragmatic terms very little and acts on still less. This may change. Within journalism, there is a fledgling movement for "public journalism" that seeks to institutionalize ways in which the general public, rather than journalists or government officials, could help set the news agenda. There is now serious discussion of what to do when the First Amendment undermines rather than assures democracy. Cass Sunstein is among the constitutional scholars who argue that a "free market" view of free speech and press can stand in the way of promoting deliberative democracy. He points to policy options consistent with democracy that might be tried out: mandating by law a right of reply in newspapers, for instance, or even establishing content-neutral government subsidies to newspapers that provide in-depth coverage of political issues.

These are encouraging developments. If they can be faulted, it is only that they still tend to treat news as information. That may be as mistaken in the long run as to take news as ideology. News is culture. To develop this notion consistently, the question would be not whether we have more or less news but what kind of news it is we have. And it is not a matter of deciding the impact of news on democracy (or democracy on news) but the mutually constitutive character of both.

Our moral destiny turns, William James said, on "the power of voluntarily attending." But he recognized, a century ago, that these acts of voluntary attention are "brief and fitful." Even so, he argued, they are all-important to our individual and collective destinies. In a way, James was only echoing Tocqueville, who observed that "even when one has won the confidence of a democratic nation, it is a hard matter to attract its attention."

Can the media help people pay more attention? This is one of two questions that the media should be asking themselves. The other question is: In the *absence* of wide readership or mass viewership, how can the media improve democracy? If the media cannot by themselves entice an audience to attend to public issues, if most of the time most people will have better things to do than watch the news or read the front page, can the media still serve a democratic function? Congress itself still faces the problem of attention: How can congressional representatives make reasonably informed votes on issues where they have not been able to inform themselves? What happens in practice is that legislators do not gather information so much as they "take cues" as they vote on complex issues about which they are largely ignorant. They follow the lead of better informed, trusted colleagues whom they would probably agree with if they had time to make independent evaluations themselves.

It will not do to blame the victim, the underinformed citizen, for the failures of American democracy. Nor will it suffice to blame the messenger, the media burdened with greater expectations than they could ever meet. The structure of our polity and our parties are implicated. The fabric of our everyday lives at home, work, church and school, on the freeway and in the supermarket, at the Little League game or on the street, is involved.

The news serves a vital democratic function whether in a given instance anyone out there is listening or not. The news constructs a symbolic world that has a kind of priority, a certification of legitimate importance. And that symbolic world, putatively and practically, in its easy availability, in its cheap, quotidian, throw-away material form, becomes the property of all of us. That is a lesson in democracy in itself. It makes the news a resource when people are ready to take political action, whether those people are ordinary citizens or lobbyists, leaders of social movements or federal judges. This is the necessity and the promise of the public knowledge we call news and the political culture of which it is an essential part.

Michael Schudson, a 1985–86 Media Studies Center fellow, is professor of communication and sociology at the University of California, San Diego. This chapter is adapted from his most recent book, The Power of News *(Harvard University Press, 1995).*

6

Maoism *vs.* Media in the Marketplace

Orville Schell

What makes China such a perplexity at the end of the 20th century is that it is an unending series of contradictions. Central to almost all of these contradictions is a single anomaly: At the same time that Deng Xiaoping's sweeping reforms had been releasing economic life from central strictures to operate according to market forces, the Chinese Communist Party had also been tightening its Maoist grip on politics in an effort to pre-empt any serious political dialogue and opposition from arising. "Letting go" *(fang)* in the economic realm while "tightening up" *(shou)* in the political realm has created a cognitive dissonance and a dialectical tension that makes China both exciting and uncertain. Nowhere is this excitement and tension more evident than in the country's booming media where the imperatives of the free market are coming into their own even as an autocratic leadership attempts maintaining a closed, one-party political system. But just as the pressure of one geologic plate against another creates earthquakes, it is possible that China's increasingly market-driven media will ultimately collide with its stubbornly resistant, Leninist state in a politically tectonic way.

Whether this happens depends on a whole host of factors, some of which are unique to China. The outcome is important not only because it will help determine the future of this latter-day People's Republic, but because it will also shed light on the validity of a core assumption underlaying recent American policy towards China, namely, that open

markets lead by their very nature to democratization and open societies without other kinds of more direct international pressure being
brought to bear. There is no better way to examine this supposition
than by studying China's existing media control apparatus and how
publishing, broadcasting and film-making are being effected by emerging free-market forces.

China's system of media control, which was originally adopted
from Stalinist Russia in the 1950s, works primarily through "Party
branches" located in every media outlet. The print press is now also
overseen by the State General Publishing Administration under the
control of Party Central Committee's Propaganda Department, while
the electronic media and film industry fall under the aegis of the
Ministry of Radio, Film, and Television. What officials within these
control organizations are discovering, however, is that as China's
economy is put ever more on a market basis, as state subsidies are
reduced and the survival of media outlets grows more dependent on
income from advertising rather than on political rectitude, and as China
fragments into increasingly self-sufficient regional economic units, central control is being challenged and a revolution in media programming is occurring.

Sometimes this unusual transformation finds expression in illegal
and quasi-legal ways. In the book and magazine industry, for instance,
private underground publishers comprising what is known as the "second channel" have arisen. Their *modus operandi* is to surreptitiously
buy or steal *shuhao* (official "book registration numbers") from legitimate state publishers and then to sell their publications through independent commercial networks that involve renegade printers, entrepreneurial distributors and private street peddlers. Most second-channel
products are not very edifying—tawdry books, magazines and tabloids
which exploit previously taboo subjects such as fashion, crime, sex,
pornography, personal finance, fortunetelling, martial arts and the su-
pernatural. But they have introduced the reading public to a new diversity of choices, and as the historian Robert Darnton has pointed out
in his studies of pre-revolutionary France, even such genres as pornography, by placing emphasis on individual choice, can have profound
repercussions for entrenched authority. Recently, China's 548 officially sanctioned publishing houses were reported to have put out 6.2
billion copies of 104,700 different books. However, nobody really
knows the number of second-channel volumes that unofficially en-

tered the market place. The same is true of fly-by-night magazines, thousands of which appear for a few issues and then vanish like puffs of steam before authorities can crack down on their producers.

Because it has become almost impossible for Party watchdogs to keep on top of the situation, some culturally *outre* and politically dissident publications have appeared, and even enjoyed significant sales before ultimately being noticed and banned. But here there is a paradox at work. For at the same time that the market has undeniably created a new latitude in publishing, with the bottom line become the new supreme standard of success, vulgar pulp offerings have hit China like a *tsunami,* making it ever more difficult for serious works to find outlets. As a result, publications with real intellectual and political content have tended to be squeezed out, proportionally diminishing the national political dialogue.

Large dailies remain under even tighter political control than book-publishing houses. Like other state enterprises, however, they also are now being weaned off the state dole, and therefore are being forced to pay attention to profits and losses as never before. This means selling ads. With some 30,000 agencies creating $13.4 billion in annual revenues (a figure that is increasing at approximately 40 percent a year), the advertising industry is now one of China's hottest economic sectors. Even papers directly under Party control such as the *People's Daily* have long since started selling ad space (sometimes on page one!), and even to expand in the lucrative world of tabloid publishing by putting out racy Sunday magazines and weeklies. What makes it so difficult for the old organs of censorship to control these phenomena is that the very officials charged with ideological supervision now often have a financial stake in the commercial success of the very publications they are supposed to be regulating.

The electronic media, however, have recently become China's major vector of news and information. As such, their content is subject to a level of close Party supervision that is more comprehensive than that which is extended to other media. However, since the Politburo issued its seminal 1983 decision, "On the Programming of Radio and Television," calling for a new "four-tier development policy" allowing for the approval of various levels of locally funded electronic media, scores of new commercial radio stations such as Shanghai's Eastern Radio have appeared on the scene, including an AM talk-and-news station and an FM music station. Eastern now even offers several programs produced by foreign-based firms. ("Hello From Britain" and the "Sony Double Countdown" are produced by the British firm Window Communications.)

Although still organized and controlled by government officials, these market-driven upstarts have evolved kinds of programing once unheard-of in China. With competition for advertising revenues between stations heightened, they have begun to broadcast a previously unimaginable variety of fare such as programs of Western pop music announced by overseas DJs, experts giving consumer tips, call-in talk shows offering advice to the lovelorn and reports on China's two stock markets. Broadcasts have certainly become ever more lively, but like Marcel Marceau trapped within his invisible glass box, producers and hosts remain constrained by unwritten but inviolable taboos against delving into politically sensitive topics.

Although there are absolute limits to what can be broached and said on the air, China's new kinds of radio programming are nonetheless making listeners accustomed to hearing ordinary people express themselves in public, a phenomenon that was formerly out of the question in "People's China." At the same time, the fierce competition for advertisers that this new diversity of stations is engendering has forced even once-stodgy Radio Beijing and Radio Shanghai to pay attention to listener preferences and demands. Radio Shanghai now has six stations, including an English-language pop music channel—Shanghai Calling—that has started to broadcast shows originating outside of China such as "Easy AM," produced in Australia, and "Joy AM," produced in Hong Kong. Whereas once there was little diversity in broadcasting, now people have some variety. Such pluralism, even though it does not yet have a really overt political dimension, has injected a whole new dynamic into China's rapidly evolving broadcast industry.

Like radio, over the past decade Chinese television has also been undergoing a process of rapid mitosis. Whereas once there was only the national network, Central Chinese Television (CCTV), which was complemented by individual municipal channels in provinces and certain large cities, now a whole variety of new stations has burst forth onto the scene. Responding in the late 1980s to the same four-tier development policy that presaged the decentralization and growth of radio stations, local investors (mostly government agencies and state-owned enterprises with an entrepreneurial eye) began setting up for-profit television ventures in their own jurisdictions. The new slogan was: "Those who invest, should benefit." Whereas in 1978 China had only 32 TV stations, by 1992 the number had skyrocketed to 591. Almost all of the new arrivals were locally based. Moreover, many localities also began approving so-called "educational channels" to operate in a curious shadowland between the public and the private sectors. The educational channels were sponsored by local commissions and chartered to put on "educational" programming, but since they are also largely dependent on commercial advertising for survival, they too heed the laws of supply and demand. And nothing seems to create demand in China like foreign programming. Although the Chinese have acquired a good deal of foreign programming over the years on a barter basis, by making commercial time available to foreign producers, in recent years a veritable stampede of foreign television programmers has hit China, as the likes of Ted Turner's TBS Far East, Rupert Murdoch's News Corporation, Time Warner Inc.'s Warner Music Group and many smaller production companies have turned their attention to this crypto-People's Republic. It seems likely that the next phase of China's electronic media "counter-revolution" will involve an increasing amount of foreign and joint-venture programing.

Two other phenomena are helping to rapidly change Chinese television. The first is the introduction of satellites. Not only have the Chinese bought transponders on foreign satellites to improve CCTV transmission to remote areas, but now they are launching their own. Apstar-1 was put in orbit in July 1994, but Apstar-2's Long March rocket blew up under it in January 1995, dealing a temporary blow to Chinese plans for becoming a major player in the industry. Nonetheless, as of 1993 the number of satellite receiving stations in China had grown 40–fold since 1987 (from 4,609 to over 40,000), making most of China's 1.2 billion people citizens of the global TV village. As of 1994, the Chinese had some 230 million TV sets with 800 million viewers, and CCTV alone was offering four nationwide channels. But quantity does not equal quality, especially when it comes to political discourse. Because programming is still under the tight political control of the Party, even though ever larger numbers of Chinese are watching TV, the level of political discourse offered—especially when it comes to sensitive topics like human rights, freedom of expression, or multiparty politics—remains low.

The second phenomenon that is pushing China into the electronic information age is foreign satellite transmissions from overseas networks such as Murdoch's Hong Kong-based Star TV that now broadcasts five channels (one in Mandarin) across 38 nations in Asia, including China, and the Middle East. When Murdoch bought into Star TV in August 1993 and not only made a number of bold anti-authoritarian utterances but put the BBC's World Service Television News on the air, many wondered if he was going to challenge Beijing's political control of the airwaves over China. However, when the Chinese government began complaining about the BBC's reports on China (insisting that they "hurt the feelings of the Chinese people"), Murdoch announced that he would take the news off the air in favor of Mandarin-language entertainment programming. Although his decision had the appearance of being in response to political pressure, some media analysts pointed out that it also had a commercial logic, namely, to win a larger share of the Chinese-speaking market with more popular Mandarin-language programming.

Fearing further encroachment by foreign satellite transmissions, in October 1993 the Chinese government moved to impose a ban on receiving dishes that had begun springing up like mushrooms all across China. Although nobody quite knew how many of these technically illegal dishes there were in China, by 1994 estimates ranged upwards to 1 million. Not only were individuals watching Star TV, which comes in over Asiasat (ironically the same satellite that carries CCTV transmissions), but enterprising private entrepreneurs were soon also hooking up whole buildings, work compounds, and even neighborhoods to dishes in what has become a whole web of *de facto* mini-cable networks.

The government has been concerned about these developments on two levels. First, it is wary of allowing heretical political ideas to leak into China via these new uncontrollable foreign vectors of information. Second, it wants to preserve its ability to monopolize all signals entering the country so that it can profit from them by selling commercials itself. After all, China got no percentage of ad revenues paid to Murdoch in Hong Kong. But instead of enforcing its ban against satellite dishes that could pick up foreign programming, officials have adopted a surprising but very astute alternative policy: They have turned to glutting the Chinese viewing public with politically acceptable home-grown programming. The effect of this policy has been both to increase the number of indigenous wireless broadcast stations within China and to encourage the setting up of a whole trove of domestic cable companies. Shanghai Cable TV, for instance, now has four channels (with eight more in the works) and is already showering its 1.2 million subscribers (who pay a 225–*yuan* ($28) installation fee and an 8–*yuan* ($1) monthly service charge) with Western pop music, sports and soap operas. Eastern Radio has now even started to move into cable television. It recently rented one of Shanghai Cable's 12 channels to create an MTV-like cable pop music outlet.

The Chinese film world is also evolving rapidly. At this point, however, it is still bizarrely segmented into three more-or-less distinct blocs. The first is made up of directors like Chen Kaige and Zhang Yimou, who use overseas capital to make art-house productions for foreign consumption. Because these films are often of high artistic quality and sometimes suggestively political, they usually end up being banned at home. The second bloc is comprised of local directors who make films with domestic funds from officially approved scripts for Chinese consumption. Their works are usually of poor artistic quality, politically neutered and viewed by an increasingly small and unenthusiastic home-theater audiences. The third block is made up of renegade underground directors such as Zhang Yuan, He Jianjun and Zhou Xiaowen, who raise their own funds within China from private entrepreneurs to make low-budget, avant-garde films. These are almost always banned at home and usually end up being screened only at film festivals abroad, where they provoke angry protests from the Chinese government.

Despite the ways the Chinese media outlets have multiplied during the last few years, party officials still retain ample means to censor and ban, as well as to arrest those individuals whom they perceive as political threats. As a result, even in this newly-marketized media environment where profit is coming to rule, most decision-makers assiduously continue to avoid politically controversial subjects. After all, getting in trouble with party watchdogs over sensitive topics rarely helps the bottom line. So for now there is a strange calm between these potentially antagonistic forces.

There may come a time, however, when the Party's loss of financial control over the media and the lure of profits will combine with unplanned circumstances (such as a leadership struggle, hyper-inflation, worker unrest or other political disturbances) to goad more adventuresome entrepreneurs into taking a more overtly independent posture in their news coverage and programming. Such was certainly the case in 1989, when the media actually did throw off the yoke of Party censorship for a week or so to become a vector for serious political reportage. And, not to be forgotten, its coverage attracted some of the highest ratings in Chinese history. Nowadays, even Party hard-liners know that such ratings equal profits that may someday become irresistible.

Such a conclusion is not a certainty, however, at least in the immediate future. Given the government's ongoing control of political content, it is still far from clear whether market forces in China are liberating the media to become a voice of free expression, or whether they are simply liberating it within the confines of the Leninist state to make more money. The latter has certainly been Deng Xiaoping's vision. Moreover, it has certainly not escaped the notice of official policy-makers that soporific trash is not only profitable, but also has a powerfully anesthetic effect on the masses. The Party, whose main *raison d'etre* is to retain unilateral political power, could do worse for its cause than turn China into a nation of tabloid-dazed couch potatoes. From the standpoint of free expression, such a result would, of course, be a disappointment. It would also be a bitter irony that would necessitate a re-evaluation of the comforting notion that free markets alone are sufficient to induce open societies.

Orville Schell, dean of the Graduate School of Journalism at the University of California, Berkeley, is a Media Studies Center senior fellow. He is an author and journalist who has written extensively about China and Asia, whose latest book is Mandate of Heaven.

7

Transforming Television in India

Sevanti Ninan

Change is the defining characteristic of the Indian media today. It is rapid, continuous and the result of two major developments: economic reform, which has led to a substantial opening of the Indian market, and the advent of transnational satellite television broadcasting in Asia. Both happened in 1991 and their convergence and subsequent feeding upon each other have resulted in extraordinary transformations.

Indian television, which was totally state-controlled for three decades, has been the most dramatically affected. Until 1991 India had only one state-owned network, Doordarshan, with two channels. Today, it has more than 13 channels available via satellite and cable, including a movie channel introduced by the state-owned network. A country restricted until recently to considerably censored television news suddenly has three other news options, all independently produced, one of which is on the state-owned network. Doordarshan news, which has been described by foreign journalists as perhaps the dullest in the world—worse even than what the Soviets used to have—is still dreadfully dull, but you don't have to watch it any more.

And a nation which until 1991 was confined to perhaps one carefully-monitored weekly business program now has five daily business programs and several weekly ones, including stock- market roundups, across different channels. The business programming boom is a direct outcome of the rapid opening up of the Indian market. (For decades, India had a pseudo-socialist economy, where potential investors had to first negotiate a forest of licenses and clearances; following a conscious decision by the present government, elected in 1991, to undertake economic reform, investing in India has become much easier.) Finally, there are news and business programs on the satellite-delivered BBC channel which are international rather than national in nature.

Until now, Indian democracy had been kept vibrant by a vigilant press much more than by television. Educated Indians who read newspapers did not feel the absence of freedom of information on TV. But the rest of the country was, for profound reasons, relegated to watching a flawed state network. In a country where there is poverty and illiteracy, television is a far more influential medium than print. The recurring cost of a newspaper is relatively high for a poor family. Newspapers are confined to urban areas, but the majority of the population is rural. And while newspapers are useful if you can read, 45 percent of the Indian population is still illiterate.

Following economic reform, the market has also had an impact on the print media: Economic newspapers have grown fatter with new investment sections and other special features. Main-line dailies have responded to the competition from television with bigger and brighter color supplements on weekends, and much frothier, personality- and gossip-oriented coverage. Indian newspapers used to be obsessed with politics, but now business journalism has come into its own.

Yet these trends that follow upon the opening up of the economy and the advent of transnational TV do not add up to a drastic change in direction for the print media as a whole. The changes in print journalism have been relatively small compared to changes in television.

Over the last six years, the revolution in Indian television has created a climate for greater freedom of information for the vast majority. It has created space on television for all political parties and not just the ruling party, as was the case when Doordarshan had a monopoly. Thanks to the new television, Indians are interested in business issues and the stock market, and Asia is interested in the Indian economy. Unfortunately, however, there has also been a massive boom in film-based programming and an overturning of all the priorities of public-service television. Television, which was started in India to help remedy underdevelopment, is now preoccupied with commercial programming.

The change began in 1991, when a Hong Kong-based private broadcast network called Star TV started telecasting to several Asian countries from a clutch of transponders aboard a satellite called Asiasat 1. Its mainstay was recycled American programming, but to Indian television audiences reared for three decades on the dreariest of indigenous fare, it was like manna from Hollywood, if not Heaven.

Star TV found an instant reception in India because the Gulf war earlier that year had catalyzed a cable revolution in the country. Almost overnight small entrepreneurs bought satellite dishes, connected them to VCR cableheads and gave people cable connections in the big cities so that they could watch the war in their drawing rooms. When the war ended they showed Hindi movies on these cable channels and got an even bigger response. When Star TV came, they went in for multichannel cables.

In every city there had been hundreds of video parlors—shops that rented out movies on videocassette. These changed overnight into small-time cable operators offering CNN and Star TV's five channels, which included the BBC and MTV. They would merely buy thousands of yards of cable and link up all the homes in the neighborhood that wanted to subscribe to their satellite dish and VCR system. It yielded an instant multichannel Nirvana for a society bred on state-owned TV. It was thoroughly innovative and thoroughly illegal, for overhead cable connections were forbidden under existing state laws.

Much of the broadcasting revolution in India over the last four years has ridden on this illegal network of cable systems, which proliferated rapidly and now covers many small towns and even villages. Only in March 1995 was legislation finally enacted, regularizing cable and prescribing norms to be observed. But even before this, the state had itself cheerfully participated in the illegality by launching satellite channels which it hoped these operators would carry.

It is important to emphasize here that compared to some other countries in Asia, the Indian government's response to this invasion from the skies was inherently democratic. It did not even attempt a ban on satellite dishes, as has been the case in say, China and Malaysia. (Star TV had to drop the BBC channel from its northern beam covering China in 1993 on account of pressure from the Chinese government.) India is too huge, its population too scattered, and democracy too ingrained in it for such a ban to ever have been effective.

Also, this media invasion did not threaten the essential nature of government because India is not a closed society. In late 1992 the

BBC channel's director in Hong Kong claimed that his channel had helped restore democracy in Thailand that year. No such grandiose claims can be made about the effect of satellite TV on India. Nevertheless, a whole series of changes in broadcasting and society have occurred as a result of the media ferment unleashed by this phenomenon.

The first of these was greater freedom of information over television. Here was a country with a feisty press whose only television network was always found wanting when the news was momentous. When Indira Ghandi was assassinated by her own security guards in 1984, Indians had to tune into BBC radio to get confirmation of the event because newspapers could only give the news the next morning. When her son was assassinated seven years later, there was a terse passing mention on a late-night bulletin, after which the state-owned Doordarshan network signed off till the next morning! When a mosque alleged to have been built on the site of a Hindu temple was pulled down by Hindu fanatics in December 1992—a watershed event in India's turbulent communal history—Doordarshan's cameras were there to record the event, but the prime minister's office intervened to ensure that the footage was never shown.

Despite these limitations, television and radio have long been important sources of information in India because they cross barriers of poverty and literacy. It was primarily to combat poverty, illiteracy, disease and backwardness that television was introduced in India in 1959. In fact, until satellite TV came to India with its varied programming, TV was essentially a medium for the poor. The first telecasts were for schools, and subsequently there came telecasts for farmers. Even today the poor and those dwelling in rural areas get their news from it, but do not necessarily buy the government propaganda that comes with it.

A single television system can also reach far more people than a single newspaper. Doordarshan, even with its numerous limitations, has in the late '80s and in the '90s played a bigger agenda-setting role than all the major newspapers in the country put together. For close to ten years or more, prime-time television spots have preached the importance of family planning, immunization and giving equal status to female children. (Boys are valued in Indian society to the extent that there is often criminal neglect of girls.) In the same period, communal conflicts in the country have also been addressed on television through fiction and public service spots, though no one knows for sure with how much effect.

The better-off, on the other hand, considered it mostly beneath them to watch Doordarshan's dreary offerings and its censored news. They watched movies on their VCRs, and the odd evening-television drama, but by and large they did not get hooked onto television until the satellite channels came.

Since late 1988 Indians have learned to turn to monthly video newsmagazines—which were spawned by leading publishing houses and circulated via public subscription—for independent footage of striking news events. These were a peculiarly Indian phenomenon and flourished for the next few years. Meanwhile, satellite TV brought a BBC news channel in 1991, so that when the mosque was destroyed Indians all over the country tuned in anxiously to the BBC. They also waited for the video magazines to give their version of this event, though these were duly censored under film censorship laws.

But the expansion of independent broadcasting has provided Indians with alternatives to such restricted fare. In 1994 Zee TV, a Hindi satellite channel part-owned by Rupert Murdoch, began a popular program which featured interviews with Indian politicians. This had been attempted twice on Doordarshan long before, but both attempts had quickly come to grief under pressure from politicians opposed to such instant accountability. This program, however, proved vastly popular and succeeded in attracting several important figures.

Doordarshan inevitably had to respond. In early 1994, as a first step, two leading video magazines—"Newstrack" and "Eyewitness"—were allowed to come onto the state network, Doordarshan, as weekly current affairs programs. There were constant battles over what could be permitted on these and what could not, but the programs survive and have developed a faithful following.

However, these could soon become irrelevant because by 1995, several daily news options had become available to the Indian viewer. Doordarshan has responded to market competition by permitting a private broadcaster to present a daily English news bulletin on one of its two terrestrial channels. In March 1995 its biggest satellite competitor, Zee TV, began a daily news show that comes on at exactly the same time as Doordarshan's prime evening bulletin—and gives far more space to the political opposition than the state channel does. And April 1995 saw the launching of the first news channel of Indian origin, via satellite, from a private broadcaster owned by a publishing house.

The sobering aspect of all this competition, though, is that satellite TV is still largely an urban middle-class phenomenon, and so this plurality of news sources is still only for the few. Satellite TV reaches 10 million households, compared to Doordarshan's reach of 40 million households. But in some parts of the country, such as the more developed western states of Gujarat and Maharashtra, satellite TV has already begun to penetrate villages. It is a process that can only accelerate.

Yet another unusual result of a market-driven satellite TV boom has been the export of Indian democracy to other countries in the Asian region. Star TV may reach 50 countries Asia wide, as it likes to say in its television promotionals, but the truth is that the only one that matters as a market for this pan-Asian broadcaster is India. It has the largest middle class—the much-touted 200 million that corporations all over the world are homing in on. It is also an increasingly acquisitive middle class that advertisers want to reach. There is no better bet for Star TV, which is losing its majority owner Rupert Murdoch several million dollars a year, than to target India as a source of advertising revenues.

But wooing India has meant working to keep the Indian government happy. To date, the Indian prime minister has been the only Asian leader invited to take questions from all over the world over a live televised hookup on Star TV's BBC channel. He is certainly the Asian leader whose speeches are televised live most frequently to the entire Asian region. On India's independence day, Republic Day, and even on Budget Day, when the Indian budget is presented in Parliament, Star TV routinely carries the proceedings live. And Zee TV, not to be outdone, came to the ruling party's rescue in 1994 when it wanted to telecast a party rally nationwide, but was precluded by telecast codes from using the national broadcaster, Doordarshan, to do so. Suddenly you had a pan-Asian TV channel carrying live the political party event of a single country.

It is also important to note that the fact that Star TV carries—on two different channels—two weekly business programs on India certainly helps India advertise abroad that it is a rapidly deregulating economy. In addition, Zee TV carries a weekly business program on India and a daily program on the Indian stock market. It has a substantial viewership among expatriate Indians and Pakistanis in the Gulf, an audience that the Indian government is only too happy to reach. In 1995, for example, the Indian government bought time on Zee TV's transponder to begin an external service aimed at the Gulf and other South Asian countries.

So at the end of six years of rapid change in Indian television, rivals are becoming collaborators, the viewer has choice and there is a tremendous race among competing channels to grab advertising. So is everything well? Not really.

Thanks to competition from foreign satellite channels, Doordarshan, which used to be essentially a public service broadcaster, has turned unrecognizably commercial, partly to retain audiences and partly because the present government has drastically cut budgetary support, expecting Doordarshan to earn its way as India becomes more and more of a market economy.

While programming for schools and farmers persists to this day, these offerings are allocated shoestring budgets and are pushed off the air when sponsored presentations like cricket matches have to be accommodated. Meanwhile on prime time, soap operas, sitcoms and films reign. Doordarshan's latest stab at winning viewers away from competing channels has been a film channel. The fact that this can be a priority in a country where a third of the population (some 300 to 360 million people in a population of 950 million) still live at subsistence level is an indication of the waywardness of the television revolution.

A great deal has changed in India and its television because of technological invasion from abroad. The changes have been complex, but in broad terms they demonstrate that competition can bring a plurality of information and entertainment sources. Foreign competition anxious to ingratiate itself with a country's government and viewership can also help project that country's image positively beyond its borders. At the same time, however, market-oriented competition can skew a nation's priorities, further marginalizing segments of society that are already on the margin. It is a remarkably sane nation that can maximize the gains and minimize the dangers. Indian policy makers are still groping for the right balance.

Sevanti Ninan is television critic for The Hindu *in New Delhi, India. She is the author of* Change Maker: Television and Change in Indian Society.

8

The Price of African Press Freedom

Joe Davidson

Freedom of the press is a noble notion. But that freedom is not available for free—especially in much of Africa. For many, the economic and political costs of creating a free press are just too high to pay. Entry into a monopolized media market, such as is the norm in many poor countries, requires a financial base that simply is not there. And the opposition from governments, even those espousing free-press rhetoric, can make attempts to push for an independent press a personally risky business.

All this is true in Africa. Yet there are important lessons to be learned there, where many nations are seeking to transform their closed political and economic structures into ones that are more open, democratic and people-friendly. The news is both good and bad.

Though such efforts well precede this decade, the 1990s have seen an intensification of movements to bring about multiparty democracies in Africa. With these have come a variety of strategies to use more market-oriented tools to stimulate moribund economies. African movements for democracy have not achieved a straight line of successes. Some nations' economic policies have led to significant turmoil. Nonetheless, the direction seems clear: Democracy and free market economies will grow. Growing pains, however, including squabbles over press freedom, will continue to be part of the process.

African media operating in a context of emerging democracy and economic liberalization face numerous problems. How can journalists

51

distribute a newspaper in a desperately poor, war-ravaged land? What does a newspaper do when it helps to bring down a one-party government only to face even greater harassment from the new, democratically elected administration? Can radio break the barriers of illiteracy and bring the news and free expression to people who cannot read newspapers and magazines? We can learn much from African journalists' efforts to overcome such challenges.

The five-year-old *mediaFAX* of Mozambique is a testimony to the ingenuity of journalists with the drive, but seemingly not the resources, to produce an independent publication. What they lacked in resources, however, they more than made up for with resourcefulness. They started a paper distributed by facsimile. "We wanted to start a weekly newspaper," said Fernando Lima, one of the founders of the paper, "but we didn't have money for newsprint and money for a printing press."

Publishing a paper by fax is a remarkable achievement in one of the world's poorest countries that is moving towards a more liberal economy. Its continued success and influence demonstrate what can be done in other places where basic survival needs such as food and shelter are given priority over press-freedom issues.

At four pages, five days a week, *mediaFAX* doesn't come cheap. The $50 monthly subscription rate equals the $600 annual income of the average Mozambican. It's like an American paying a $2,000 monthly subscription fee. The average Mozambican, of course, can't afford the Portuguese-language *mediaFAX*. But its readership apparently goes well beyond those on the subscription list, according to Lima. The paper, he said, is so widely photocopied that one vendor attributes increased copier paper sales to *mediaFAX*'s unofficial circulation.

"The official audience is the business community, the diplomatic community and the NGO (nongovernmental organization) community and the government. The nonofficial audience is almost everybody," he said in an interview. "We know of fights in institutions to get copies of *mediaFAX* in the morning." Fifty subscribers signed up in *mediaFAX*'s first month, May 1992. In the first year the subscription list grew to 500, where it remains. Five hundred paying subscribers equal a $25,000 monthly gross income for *mediaFAX,* "which gives us a lot of stability in our operation," Lima noted.

MediaFAX is produced in Maputo by Mediacoop, a group of journalists who work to ensure that the government keeps its promise of press freedom. "This was the first outlet that was not government controlled," Lima explained. Many Mediacoop members were formerly employed by the government. Today, they use sources at the top level of government to gain scoops. "They could leak this stuff to the state media," Lima told the *New York Times,* "but among the intelligentsia, it has more credibility if we publish it."

That credibility is enhanced when the news sheet is profiled in newspapers such as the *Times* and the *Christian Science Monitor* and quoted in international wire services such as Agence France-Presse (AFP). One June 1993 AFP report noted an angry parliamentarian waving a *mediaFAX* scoop about a World Bank recommendation urging Mozambique to abolish its navy and air force.

When *mediaFAX* interviewed the leader of the Mozambique National Resistance (Renamo) rebel movement, some government supporters considered the paper's publishers traitors. "We've never had something like this," Salvador Dimas, a presidential aide who has been a *mediaFAX* target, told the *Times.* "It's not progovernment, not antigovernment. It is . . ." he paused, seeking the right term to describe this new phenomenon. Independent? "Yes, independent."

While *mediaFAX* staffers have not faced the attacks journalists have suffered in other places, it has been no free ride either. A deputy minister sued the publication when it asked editorially if he was part of a stolen-car ring.

Political independence was easy for *mediaFAX* to define. Financial independence was a bit more difficult to grasp. *MediaFAX* began with help from foreign donors. "We cannot survive on donations," Lima insisted in an interview. "This will give the wrong impression to your staff. They will not care if your publication sells or does not sell. We know that donors will not be around all the time. We need to make money to have our publication succeed."

Backing has come from the business community, which supports *mediaFAX* with advertisements. In another lesson applicable to journalists elsewhere, the Mediacoop found that although business people are reluctant to criticize government officials, with whom the entrepreneurs may be closely linked, they are willing to support those in a better position to criticize and who can help the business agenda. *MediaFAX,* for example, wrote about government customs policies that hampered growing private sector development. "It's not that we are doing things to please the business sector," Lima explained, "but they see the need for a free press."

Ironically, such appreciation for free expression did not extend to a Zambian government elected on a prodemocracy platform. Fred M'membe, editor-in-chief of the *Post,* an independent biweekly, was hopeful that Zambia's first multiparty elections in 17 years would produce greater press freedom. The *Post,* after all, first appeared just three months before the 1991 vote that rejected 27–year president Kenneth Kaunda in favor of union leader Frederick Chiluba. "We never supported anybody's campaign," M'membe said. "But Chiluba's party stood for democracy. Those appearing to fight for democracy at that time seemed to be on the same side with us."

The *Post*'s aggressive and muckraking reporting before the election undoubtedly played an important role in defeating the man considered to be the father of his country. But while the Kaunda government did give the then-*Weekly Post* relatively minor headaches, they were nothing like the major pains of the Chiluba administration. Now M'membe's *Post* and Chiluba's government frequently find themselves on opposite sides of the courtroom. "I'm facing about 11 to 15 charges on a number of accounts," M'membe said. "We are in court almost every week."

President Chiluba sued the *Post* after it reported accusations made by a sacked cabinet minister that Chiluba is a marijuana smoker involved in drug trafficking. In July of 1994, the *Post* quoted former legal affairs minister Ludwig Sondashi saying he had documents to "show that Chiluba smokes dagga at State House." No other Zambian news organization reported Sondashi's charges. He was arrested and charged with impropriety and misconduct in office. The Zambian information ministry did not respond to requests for comment.

M'membe says though he doesn't know if the charges are true, the Post had a responsibility to report the accusations that were made by a credible individual during a press conference in a government building. He likens the *Post*'s coverage to reports in American media about President Clinton's alleged sexual affairs. "I felt we had a duty to report that," M'membe said. "The truth was slightly immaterial or secondary.... I do not have the capacity to investigate that. Drug trafficking is real in this part of the world. It is becoming the only profitable business."

The *Post* has paid heavily for press freedom. A *Post* delivery truck was ambushed in September 1993 just days before President Chiluba sued the paper over a story containing allegations that he had been offered a bribe to allow South African businessmen permission to organize a crocodile hunt. Gunmen stopped the van carrying 50,000 copies of the paper, assaulted the driver, burned the papers and stole the vehicle.

"There's a lot of work that has to be done," before even democratically-elected governments truly extend democratic protections to the press, observes M'membe. "And there's a lot of sacrifice that has to be taken."

Fourteen months after the ambush, police stormed through the newspaper's Lusaka offices looking for embarrassing pictures of the president, according to M'membe. "It is the first time in the history of Zambia, including the colonial history, that a newspaper was searched by police as ours was," M'membe complained. "The presses were stopped from printing until everything was searched. That raised a number of concerns regarding the freedom of the press. Our sources were exposed to the police."

The government's attitude toward the *Post* demonstrates that without adequate safeguards, a democratically-elected government will not automatically embrace press freedom. Emerging democracies sometimes retain laws, such as those which protect a president from criticism, which can be used to stifle aggressive journalism. "The march toward democracy is not matched by democratic institutions and legal and institutional reforms," M'membe said. "New democrats have a desire to protect power and negate legal and democratic reforms. They do not have a culture of tolerance. They cannot take criticism."

That intolerance comes from the lack of a strong social infrastructure in some African nations, argues Methaetsile Leepile, executive director of the Media Institute of Southern Africa, based in Windhoek, Namibia. Without that infrastructure, democracy cannot take root, he said, leaving government beyond criticism. "In our countries, if you talk about the government you are talking about God," Leepile said. "It is as if you are not talking about people. Governments have been above the people."

The belief in godlike government can be pushed more easily on an uneducated people than on a knowledgeable body politic. Illiteracy, and the ignorance that often accompanies it, can be used by those in power to maintain control. With illiteracy comparatively widespread in much of Africa, particularly in the rural areas, informing important segments of a citizenry about crucial issues can be a daunting task.

Here radio plays a crucial role. Newspapers and magazines may be inexpensive, but you have to know how to read them to get the news. That is not the case with radio. And a radio, unlike television, can run on batteries that fit in your pocket. Many people can gather around a radio to hear programs broadcast from many miles away. Radio's importance is demonstrated every time some beleaguered nation has a coup: The radio station is the first thing captured.

Governments, according to *Who Rules the Airwaves? Broadcasting in Africa,* published by Article 19 and the *Index on Censorship* in London, "may be prepared to tolerate a critical independent press while maintaining tighter control of radio, which has a much wider reach." Broadcasting is much more closely controlled by governments than print journalism.

What is needed, the report argues, is true public-service broadcasting, not merely private radio stations. "Today, the main question confronting broadcasting in East and southern Africa is how to transform government stations into genuine, independent public-service broadcasters," the editors say in the introduction. "The importance of this issue has been largely overlooked by the international community, which has concentrated instead on pressing for the legalization of private broadcasters as a means of ensuring pluralism."

Far more so than their neighbors to the north, Namibia and South Africa have taken great strides toward institutionalizing truly independent broadcasting. Namibian law guarantees the independence of the Namibian Broadcasting Corporation (NBC). And South Africa's Independent Broadcasting Authority (IBA) is licensing community radio stations that are intended to serve as a buffer between the government and the long-established, though recently much-changed, South African Broadcasting Corporation.

Since its 1990 independence, Namibia has been on the forefront of guaranteeing independence to its broadcasters. The new government dropped direct state control of NBC soon after taking office. New laws permitted private ownership of radio and television stations. Nonetheless, broadcasters still must be vigilant to keep out political interference.

"For the Corporation's critics, proof of political interference and pro-government bias in Namibian Broadcasting Corporation news and program coverage came when the Corporation recently dropped the word 'autonomous' from its mission statement," wrote David Lush of the Media Institute of Southern Africa in *Who Rules the Airwaves?*

The Namibian Broadcasting Corporation's director-general, Nahum Gorelick, asked Lush: "If we still depend on the state for 65 percent of our funding, how autonomous can we be?" Government officials tried to use that funding as leverage to get programming they favored, Gorelick added.

The state subsidy has been cut 40 percent since independence. That has forced the Namibian Broadcasting Corp. to rely more on advertising revenue, which means, according to Lush, that it caters to the "affluent white minority" that has the money to buy the advertised goods and services.

In neighboring South Africa, the IBA is busy granting licenses to small community-based radio stations designed to serve a diverse group of interests. By the end of the year, more than 60 licenses will have been given to a wide variety of organizations, ranging from a wildlife advocacy association to a Greek-language group.

Alex-FM, a station serving the impoverished Alexandra township adjacent to one of Johannesburg's more affluent neighborhoods, will provide a community beset with poor schools, dirt streets and a high illiteracy rate with news and features designed to meet the needs of previously ignored residents.

While some stations are funded by universities or religious groups, those in poor communities are backed by foundations and foreign-government donors. The stations get no South African government funding and are run on a nonprofit basis. "They can take ads," John Matisonn, an IBA counselor explained, "but they can't put the money in people's pockets." The ability to develop radio and other media outlets, then, is closely related to the strength of the South African economy, as is the case in the rest of the continent.

In many African countries, the increase in independent publications is a tangible indication of citizens' strong desire for democracy. And expanding economic structures will provide greater opportunity, through diverse sources of advertising, for independent media to grow. But the continuing, sometimes very serious, threats to press freedom demonstrate that even in countries with popularly elected governments there may be gaps between gallant rhetoric and brutal realities. The lack of enforced statutory guarantees and, perhaps more importantly, a tradition of government interference with the media, means there will be more problems before press freedom is a widespread certainty.

Such struggles, of course, are not unique to Africa. One must simply recall history lessons about the violence visited upon some newspapers during earlier days in the United States of America. Young nations, as those in Africa are, can learn from their youthful, reckless deeds and grow to sustain the kind of press freedom that people want. The cup is at least half full.

Joe Davidson covers criminal justice and immigration for the Wall Street Journal *in Washington and has been reporting on Africa since 1986.*

9

Magic Realism in Latin America

María Luisa MacKay

In novels written in the style of magic realism, anything can happen. And in Latin America, the cradle of this literary genre, the same holds true for journalism.

A democratically elected president accuses reporters of "journalistic delinquency" in the middle of a press conference? It happened not long ago in Argentina.

Radio stations are bombed, journalists are murdered, and almost none of the cases are solved? It happens in Colombia.

A powerful media group creates a presidential candidate and two years later contributes to his fall and impeachment? It happened in Brazil.

Scandals, untold secrets and power games—all exaggerated and amplified without limits. That's politics and journalism in Latin America.

In the last decade a wave of democratization swept the subcontinent, yet many of these young democracies are still learning how to walk properly. The political systems work, in many cases, like new shoes—they hurt, they press in the wrong places and still provoke painful blisters.

On this troubled planet, Latin America is considered a more-or-less peaceful region, but any other generalization could be dangerous. In Latin America you can find everything from tight censorship, as in Peru, to detailed reporting of the fall of a president, as in the case of Fernando Collor de Mello in Brazil.

Latin America is a place where reporters still struggle to expose abuses of power, a place where every year reports from organizations such as the Committee to Protect Journalists (CPJ) and Amnesty International list attacks or threats against journalists and the media.

According to a CPJ report, Peru has blazed a path—and it is not shining or luminous—to having the most imprisoned journalists in Latin America. Ten reporters are now serving prison terms under anti-terrorism laws, CPJ reported in 1995. The government of Alberto Fujimori has released 12 journalists jailed under terrorism charges since 1992, but a new monitoring organization, Instituto Prensa y Sociedad, has since then listed another 13 cases with sentences of up to 20 years.

Colombia is also treacherous terrain for journalists in the region. Reporters face many different hostile fronts at the same time. Over the last 15 years, according to the Latin American chapter of CPJ, guerrillas, paramilitary groups and drug traffickers have killed up to 50 reporters and a powerful Colombian tradition of investigative reporting.

A decree issued by President Ernesto Samper Pizano has forbidden print and broadcast interviews with guerrilla groups and drug traffickers. Meanwhile, the lords of the drug cartels are said to own at least six radio stations (some sources say more than a dozen).

More astonishing, a study by the Florida International University found that in Peru and Colombia 300 journalists have been killed over the past decade.

This is a region ruled by democratically elected governments but still wracked by political violence, narcotics trafficking, economic crises and lack of controls in the power structure. But for the press, the main problem has been the slim opportunity to practice and to experience broad freedom of expression.

The pervasive legacy of the authoritarian past means in many cases that democracy has not brought real freedom of speech. Imaginative governments can silence the press with censorship laws of all kinds. Each country has nuanced norms—call them defamation, libel, respect for honor, licenses, public interest, security laws, whatever—which have proved effective in controlling excessive enthusiasm in the reporting of public affairs.

Mandatory licensing, or *colegiación,* is becoming a new trend. Chile recently approved the system which requires journalists to have a degree and register before the *colegio.* Venezuela has passed a new law that imposes three-to-six-month prison sentences on journalists working without a license. In Brazil, the licensing law imposed by the military in the '60s is ignored in practice but still in effect. *Colegios* also exist in Costa Rica, Bolivia, Ecuador and Peru, where they vary in their operation. Although journalists within *colegios* may appreciate the economic benefits of membership—they help to insure a favorable labor market—some owners and managers consider them a hindrance. And to many writers, especially those outside the *colegio* system, they appear to be dedicated to the control of reporters rather than their defense.

After decades of dictatorships, *coups* and institutional breakdowns, people still don't fully trust their governments. An epidemic of political cynicism has led to a crisis of representation: Citizens with grievances do not approach their elected officials, but instead address their complaints and claims to the media. Common people, rather than write to a legislator, will turn to radio or TV stations in the hope that someone will answer their needs.

The electronic media often criticize city council decisions and carry an increasing number of complaints about deficient services like the lack of traffic lights. Newspapers, whose freedoms may vary dramatically from country to country, print stories about corruption and political abuses.

But in societies where nobody seems prepared to fulfill their roles, the media are no exception. Too often their stories lack full investigation, proper fact-checking or appropriate follow-ups. A call from the top may cause the most scandalous article to disappear from the newspaper pages overnight. "The investigative journalist of a major newspaper—especially one working on the political, economic or police desk—knows how often there are 'orders from above' not to touch this or that subject, to drop the mention of a name rather than run the risk of annoying a political supporter, the government or an important commercial backer," Homero Alsina Thevenet, editor of the newspaper *El País* of Montevideo, Uruguay, observed in *Index on Censorship*.

Uruguayan newspapers stand out in the region for the tendency to support openly specific political parties. In the rest of Latin America close ties between the media and the political and economic powers may be more subtle, but they are still easy to find. Such is the case in Venezuela, where media are often part of large business groups and nearly 20 journalists sit in Congress. A similar situation can be found in Brazil, where a third of congressional members have financial interests in radio and TV, and almost a quarter of radio stations are owned by elected political officials and consequently offer a constrained approach to the news.

This lack of distance between reporters and news sources is the Achilles' heel of the Latin American press. Moreover, in many countries of the region, reporters still find the role of watchdog dangerous, forbidden or onerous.

Consider the case of Argentina. There, the shameful fall of the military dictatorship in 1982 after the defeat in the Falklands/Malvinas war, and the quick transition to democracy with the victory of radical leader Raúl Alfonsín in 1983, helped plant the seeds of investigative reporting. But it took at least five years of stable democracy for the media to start practicing the genre without fear of weakening the democratic system.

In the past six years, President Menem has criticized several stories on corruption in his administration as constituting a "dictatorship of the press." The battle between media organizations and the government heated up when Menem sent the Argentine Congress restrictive press bills to increase penalties for defamation and libel (a federal crime) and to require that every media outlet carry libel insurance worth $500,000. The bills remain frozen in Congress, where they have not even been discussed. Nevertheless, the incident was an obvious attempt to restrain the freedom of the press.

In Chile, in contrast, censorship has not been as powerful as self-censorship. There, thanks to a different political situation, the press has adopted a cautious and timid tone. Reporters never challenge the hidden power of the military over civil authorities.

During the regime of General Augusto Pinochet, between 1973 and 1990, only a few media outlets linked to the Catholic Church, like Radio Cooperativa, exposed human rights violations. Meanwhile the two leading dailies, the state-owned *La Nación* and the top-selling conservative newspaper *El Mercurio,* accepted and endorsed the government's economic reforms and ignored its violent repression of political dissent. The latter is still an untouchable subject that Chileans prefer not to discuss. "So far," recalls an attentive observer of the Chilean political scene, "you can only find one book with in-depth investigative reporting about the oppression years, *The Hidden Story of the Military Dictatorship* by Eduardo Salazar, a reporter from UPI and later the daily *La Epoca.*"

During the transition it was *La Epoca,* founded by the rising opposition to the dictatorship, which promoted criticism and contributed to the victory of the Campaign for NO, which ended Pinochet's presidency. But *La Epoca* faded once the transition to democracy was underway. Since then the paper has been sold to two different business groups that have failed to restore it to its former prominence.

Brazil is a different story. Its press, which is irreverent in style, only four years ago discovered its power to bring down an allegedly corrupt president. The influential newspaper *Fólha de São Paulo* and the weekly magazine *Veja* broke the news about the corrupt administration of Collor de Mello, but the story was driven to its climax by the immensely powerful broadcasting conglomerate Rede Globo. Two years earlier, ironically, Globo had discovered the young Collor de Mello as a candidate from the state of Alagoas.

The so-called "Brazilian Watergate," in which the press played a key role in bringing down their country's president, is widely considered a turning point for Brazilian media. Nevertheless, many still believe that it is not clear whether the credit for the toppling of Collor de Mello belongs entirely to the media. Indeed, some analysts argue that they were used as instruments by ruling elites.

The media, of course, gain prestige whenever they are able to put the political establishment in the culprit's seat. We journalists are understandably addicted to such reporting. But frequent depictions of government corruption also generate cynicism that makes the public lose interest in politics and turn instead to popular soap operas. In countries such as Brazil, Venezuela and Argentina people have become so callous towards corruption cases that the media must compete with televised entertainment programs and struggle for public attention.

Corruption is perhaps the greatest obstacle to building sustainable democracies in the region. In some cases the scale and the techniques involved threaten the very existence of democratic government. Argentines, fond of exaggeration and veterans of two hyperinflations, coined the term "hypercorruption" to describe the cancerous dishonesty in their society.

In such scenarios, journalists are free from neither the flaws that afflict their societies nor their political cynicism. This situation could soon lead to a crisis of credibility in which half of the journalists are inhibited from denouncing abuses and the other half are either suspected or falsely accused of "hidden interests." In Venezuela, the fall of president Carlos Andrés Pérez under charges of corruption is mainly attributed to José Vicente Rangel, a former politician who hosts a weekly TV program and publishes columns in two newspapers, *El Universal* and *El Diario de Caracas.* But Rangel was hardly a disinterested observer of Pérez's downfall: Rangel also applauded the army's attempt to overthrow Pérez in 1992.

In Argentina a weekly magazine, *Noticias,* recently ran an astonishing investigation. A well-known union leader who is close to the administration tried to bribe a reporter into not publishing a story. The reporter taped the conversation and afterwards *Noticias* printed the bribe attempt. The follow-up to the article was most illuminating. In the next issue, the politician gave an interview on how he had learned to bribe journalists.

The practice is hardly unknown in Latin America. In a recent poll of 328 journalists in the Andean region, 58.1 percent admitted to knowing a colleague who had accepted a bribe. Part of the explanation for the problem, according to the report, is that the low salaries paid to journalists compel them to accept payoffs "to make ends meet." In most Latin American countries the average journalist's salary rarely exceeds $400 per month.

In general, low salaries have not yet been influenced by increasing investment in the region's media. Recent economic reforms in the region, including deregulation and the privatization of telecommunications industries, have attracted capital for many economic sectors, including the press.

Cable TV has invaded the region and by itself has produced a huge flow of information, accompanied by the spread of satellite transmissions and the globalization of communications. On the average in 1994, as *The Economist* reported, cable subscriptions in the region rose by more than 20 percent. In Brazil, they jumped by 80 percent. And there is still room for cable subscription growth in Latin America. The exception, however, is Argentina, where almost half of the country's households are connected to cable systems. Indeed, the following year, cable operators in Argentina enjoyed sales of more than $1.5 billion.

The appearance of huge media conglomerates has presented the public with an enjoyable and unprecedented variety of programs. The programs do not, however, necessarily reflect a diverse array of opinions, because they are often produced by a relatively small number of owners who share similar values.

Investors, companies and programming from the United States are starting to play a significant role in these developments. A few years ago, 80 percent of the biggest Argentine cable company, Cablevision, was bought out for a record $700 million by U.S.-based TCI International Holdings Inc.

On the other hand, the process of regional integration, as in the development of Mercosur, which is intended to create a common market of Brazil, Argentina, Uruguay and Paraguay, with Chile and Bolivia as associates, has already influenced the rebirth of media businesses—at least in the southernmost part of Latin America. The first joint ventures have been launched and there have also been talks between major conglomerates about joining forces in broadcasting to reach audiences across national boundaries. According to marketing surveys some 90 percent of Latin American households have a TV set, and these households represent stellar business opportunities for these companies.

However, the economic prospects of the media in Latin America are still subject to sudden change. In this region of contrasts, the pendulum still swings very fast. The Mexican *peso* crisis, for example, smashed the so-called emerging markets and confronted regional economies with the prospect of toppling like a row of dominoes.

For those who have seen everything happen in past decades, democracy is still something precious that needs to be protected. At the same time, for too many Latin Americans, freedom of speech is considered a luxury that very few can afford.

But the seeds are there, and ambitious reporters dream of achieving the scoop of their lives that will topple a president or expose a drug cartel. In the land of magic realism everything can happen—hell and utopia alike.

María Luisa MacKay is a staff writer for Clarín, *the Buenos Aires, Argentina daily. She was a Hubert H. Humphrey Fellow at the College of Journalism at the University of Maryland, College Park, when this was written.*

10

Samizdat Goes Public

Adam Michnik

It has already been eight years since the first thin and modest issue of *Gazeta Wyborcza* was published. We are the peers of the Polish democracy, its part and ally from the very beginning. Now *Gazeta* has changed its graphic design. Instead of being modest, black or gray, with sometimes illegible print, it has become an elegant, translucent paper which attracts a reader's eye.

Gazeta's new adventure with its readers is just beginning. New questions, new challenges, new dilemmas.

I have always emphasized that I am willing to take responsibility for *Gazeta's* errors and failures, but I do not take the responsibility for its success. This success is the achievement of my colleagues, who have been able to organize a modern editorial office as an effective enterprise. My contribution is limited to the fact that I did not manage to destroy everything.

I believe it to be a good habit that in such a moment the editor in chief, even if he performs his function in a rather symbolic way, should present his personal accounting.

How did we begin? *Gazeta* was supposed to be the paper of the democratic opposition which surfaced from the underground and anonymity. On the front page we wrote down in the characteristic "Solidarity" letters the slogan, "There is no freedom without solidarity!"

The September 1990 decision of the Solidarity National Committee deprived *Gazeta* of the right to use this slogan; however, this does not change the fact that I still believe "Solidarity" to be a significant and valuable experience in my life.

Gazeta, like the Polish reality, reflected the clash of various expectations, interests and systems of values. We were descendants of Solidarity, whose ethics comprised belief in the state's sovereignty, democracy, human rights, national identity, religious freedom and emancipation of the working class.

The implementation of Leszek Balcerowicz's economic shock-therapy program, which was supported by *Gazeta,* went against public expectations linked with Solidarity's victory. We had mixed feelings about strikes and protests. We noticed their irrationality, but also the drama of Solidarity unionists from various enterprises, many of whom were our friends. Those people were deeply disappointed: Instead of a godsend, which they expected after the collapse of communism, they got a decrease of real pay and unemployment. While presenting our opinions, we also tried to reflect the point of view of the losers: the impoverished, the unemployed and the frustrated. However, even though we understood Solidarity's stand, we believed the issue of system transformation to be the top priority.

We wrote about the world in a way that nobody had ever applied, particularly about the countries in the "communist camp." We joyfully greeted Václav Havel's release from prison and the symbolic funeral of Imre Nagy. We were the first Polish paper to endorse Germans' right to live in a united country. We were enthusiastic about the fall of the Berlin Wall and the "Velvet Revolution" in Czechoslovakia. We published a special issue devoted to the struggle for freedom in Romania. We wrote a lot about Russia—the thinking, democratic, rebellious Russia.

We carefully registered the process of regaining sovereignty by the postcommunist countries, but we did not express triumphant euphoria. We sensed threats and we warned against the spirit of revenge and the explosion of nationalism. We were often criticized for this. Nevertheless, I think the bloody ethnic conflicts in the Caucasus and the Balkans, the dissolution of Czechoslovakia and Vladimir Zhirinovsky's electoral success in Russia point to the fact that we were right.

At the same time, we criticized the invasion of the language of social demagogy into politics and the economy. It is hard for me to neglect the existence of similar aggressive tendencies in Solidarity and outside the union.

The language of social demagogy has appeared within the church. I believe that stupid, primitive anticlericalism is very far from *Gazeta*'s spirit. We have always understood the meaning and value of the Catholic Church in Poland. We have also remembered the praiseworthy role of this Church during the dictatorship.

Nevertheless, we were not able to avoid conflicts with some bishops. We were excommunicated by the priests at the pulpits, compared to "barking mongrels," overtly boycotted and condemned. I believe that the reason for this can be found in the fact that we attempted to write about the Church in a normal way—as any important institution functioning in a sovereign state and pluralistic society. We wrote about a Church which—like the rest of the society—had problems with adjusting to the new situation, about a Church which is sometimes used and abused by the political parties which loudly declare their Catholicism.

I feel particularly responsible for *Gazeta*'s tone of writing about the Church. I have always believed that the Church is an inextricable component of the Polish identity, and today it should be the conscience of the democratic society. The Church was natural to me as a sign of resistance, but it was impossible for me to accept it as a sign of compulsion.

This is why I was concerned about the invasion of the Church into the sphere of the profane, the ever tougher language of crusade, and open attacks on those who think differently. I know that this is not the voice of the Church. However, I do know also that this is a voice *from* the Church, the language applied by several Catholic priests. Why is this so? The Church has always won when it spoke the language of forgiveness and reconciliation, and it has always lost when it applied the language of fundamentalism, triumphalism and fear against the world.

During the "war at the top," the in-fighting among Solidarity leadership in 1990, *Gazeta* was constantly accused of being "pink."

At that time, the spring of 1990, we thought, probably naively, that it was possible to avoid a division within the Solidarity camp. We feared that it would bring negative consequences. Now I think that this camp had to divide. However, I believe that this division could have been conducted in a better style, without the ocean of insults and slanders which Solidarity members threw at each other.

I am not without blame myself. I think that my sharp tongue and the tone of some of my articles were also responsible for the growing tensions. I wrote many vicious things about politicians, including Lech Walesa. Now I deeply regret any injustice that I did with my words. At the same time, I must add that in these polemics my emotions were kept under control by my colleagues from *Gazeta*. It is to them I owe the fact that I avoided mistakes which would have harmed many people.

We somehow underrated the possibility of post-communist circles regaining power. In 1989–90, we thought that this political formation had been placed at the historical dump site. However, after four years, they regained power. Where were the roots of our mistake?

I think we overrated the power of the anti-communist attitudes in Polish society. We underrated the strength of the post-communist circles and the power of nostalgia for the epoch, which for us was enslavement, but for others was a period of social security. And last but not least, we underrated the consequences of the self-destruction of Solidarity's image.

Gazeta has always opposed discrimination against the people from the post-communist camp. I went further while writing about this problem than my colleagues. I thought that Poland should pass from dictatorship to democracy following the "Spanish" way—without settling the scores and without revenge. This is why I avoided the tone of triumph and score-settling.

However, I must admit my other mistake. I did not think that the worst models of communist nomenclature would be revived so quickly within the post-communist formation. This greediness—in taking all possible posts, in trying to control television, in the arrogant division of spoils within the ruling coalition—this is something I did not forecast. This is why I wrote so little about specific events which illustrated the process of regaining power by the apparatchiks.

Post-communists will not stage any bloody or not-bloody St. Bartholomew's Day Massacre. But still, by transforming administration into the rule of the old nomenclature, by ignoring the principles of professionalism and non-political character of the public servants, they can destroy Polish democracy.

Independent papers should resist this phenomenon.

In other words, I believe *Gazeta* is responsible for writing the truth. All the truth. I want to conduct a dispute, but I do not want to throw stones at anyone.

It is difficult to change one's views; it is difficult for a dissident, a member of the underground to become the editor in chief of the most popular newspaper in a democratic state. The reality of democracy is so different from the world of dictatorship in which I lived from the day I was born. That world was inevitably a black and white one: Goodness struggled against evil, the truth struggled against lies, freedom staged the battle against enslavement.

In the world of democracy, the prevailing color is gray. This world is ruled by arguments which are divided and not complete, by partial and contradictory interests.

During the previous period, the main threat was complete silence; now—the noisy cacophony. Today the truth is being attacked in different ways. Today we have freedom.

Even as I am writing these words, I cannot fully believe in this. I never dreamt that I would live to see this.

However, the other side of freedom is responsibility—both legal and moral. Responsibility for words. Responsibility for man, who can be destroyed with words. We did not know this type of responsibility. Now we are learning it and it is quite difficult. One can injure with words.

It is hard to learn life in democracy. The bread and wine of democracy is your opponent. And your responsibility for his freedom. You can reject all arguments presented by the papers of the leftist and rightist extremes, but it is your primary duty to struggle for their right to formulate their arguments. And you must consider the language you use while defending them. "Speech is more than blood." Remember, you struggled for language which is aimed at communication and not at mutual insults.

The Balkan war first started in the newspapers, radio stations and television stations. Before the bullets began to kill, the words killed. Tadeusz Konwicki, an eminent Polish writer, once wrote down his writer's pledge: "I will never direct my pen against other nations." It is worthwhile to listen to Konwicki.

When we write about the Ukrainians or Lithuanians, let us look at the difficult knot of our mutual relationships from a Lithuanian or Ukrainian point of view. Let us take example from those Lithuanians and Ukrainians who have enough courage to explain the Polish point of view to their compatriots. Let us write about our neighbors with sympathy and knowledge. Our writing may not help much, but it can surely do much harm.

There are not many national minorities in Poland, but there are enough of them to build conciliation or new conflicts. *Gazeta* will always choose conciliation. That is why we will continue to publish Russian, Ukrainian, Belarusian, Lithuanian, Czech, Slovak and German authors.

Gazeta Wyborcza is a newspaper. But it is also a business. Its fate depends on the readers who decide to buy it every day and spend some money from their home budget. Some time ago it was different: It was the Communist Party Central Committee which decided, or a sympathetic sponsor, or the distributor of underground funds.

Now you must win the reader. You must convince him that your *Gazeta* is worth investing in, buying and reading. You must understand and respect the rules of the market, but, while winning the reader, you must know what you want to win him for.

Readers want "vitamin I"—information. This is why we want to be a paper of the market and why we devote a lot of space to the economy. We want to be a paper of the city, and we devote much space to local inserts. We also want to be a paper which helps people to live better and with more dignity, which is why we devote so much space to articles like the one entitled, "To give birth in a dignified way."

In short, we want to be a *Gazeta* which people will need.

But we do not want to toady to our readers. We feel that we must also present—excuse this far-reaching comparison—the spirit of the Biblical prophets. We sometimes must tell bitter and upsetting truths. We must somehow combine a businessman and the prophet Jeremiah. Jeremiah without the market results in isolation, in an ivory tower; the market without Jeremiah results in cynicism.

I am aware that I feel closer to Jeremiah than to the competent expert in the needs of the press market. Many articles recommended by me—difficult essays by Václav Havel, Leszek Kolakowski or Tzvetan Todorov—were laughed at by my colleagues from the editorial office. I understand very well that no one would buy a newspaper composed only of such texts. But on the other hand, if *Gazeta* did not publish such texts at all, I would not be able to be its editor in chief, since I believe that *Gazeta* has a double character: It combines lively information with serious public affairs articles which would fit into the most respectable European dailies.

I always wanted *Gazeta* to have a clearly defined line. It resulted from the identity of the Solidarity democratic opposition and worker's social ethics, ever present in the Polish tradition. This is the snobbery of *Gazeta Wyborcza*'s editor in chief.

It is not very elegant to quote oneself. This is why I ask your forgiveness. In November 1980, in the respectable hall of the Jagiellonian University I delivered a speech. At that time I looked for an answer to a question posed by our great poet Juliusz Slowacki: "Poland, but what Poland?"

> We answer ourselves with uncertainty: self-ruled, tolerant, colorful Poland, based on Christian values, exercising social justice, friendly toward its neighbors, ready to reach compromise and exercise moderation, realism and loyal partnership, but unable to stand enslavement, spiritual submission, spiritual subjugation. Poland full of conflicts typical for modern societies, but ruled by the principle of solidarity. Poland where intellectuals defend persecuted workers, and striking workers demand freedom for culture. Poland which talks about itself with pathos and sneer, which has been conquered so many times but was never defeated, which lost but was never a loser. Poland, which has now regained its identity, its language and its face.

This is also my answer for today. I never wanted *Gazeta* to be an organ of any political party. Our sympathies are quite clear, even though they are never voiced openly by our journalists. But we were open to all wise thoughts, regardless of who voiced them. And I do hope that it will remain the same in the future.

I have thousands of grudges against the politicians from both the Christian-National Alliance and the Alliance of the Democratic Left, but the principle of professional decency and the normal requirements of democratic order make us treat them as a normal component of Polish pluralism.

I was one of the first journalists to declare publicly that he would not vote for Lech Walesa. I voted for Tadeusz Mazowiecki. Nevertheless, I believe that *Gazeta Wyborcza*'s clear involvement during the presidential elections and its support for Mazowiecki was my personal mistake. An independent daily should not become a party in a political struggle. I can have my personal sympathies which I can reveal in *Gazeta,* but I should not treat *Gazeta* as an instrument in the electoral campaign.

I am very critical about Walesa and, at the same time, I have a lot of warm feelings for him. For the past few years I have criticized him quite often. I think he is a bad president and I believe Poland needs a different president. However, it was Lech Walesa who was elected president. And since that moment he has also become my president. I can criticize him, as the French criticized Mitterand and Americans criticize Clinton, but I must respect the head of my country. I cannot allow him to be insulted and sneered at.

It is difficult to assess his performance as a president. He has said many nonsensical things and I am afraid that he will continue to say further nonsense.

However, let us be just. During five years of his administration, Poland did not leave the way of reforms and did not stop being a democratic, law-abiding country. I would like to wish Walesa to become a part of our history in this way—as a historical leader of "solidarity," Nobel Prize winner, and defender of Polish reforms. I wish him to forget about "Yeltsin's variant," about continuing to hold his post by violating the Constitutional Act.

In the upcoming elections *Gazeta* will attempt to present objectively the arguments of all candidates. This is what our readers can expect of us, since they will vote for various candidates.

Just like all Poland, *Gazeta* enters a time of turmoil. We enter it in good condition, but full of fears. We would like to be as close to our readers, with this new graphic design, as we used to be. But let's make it clear: We will bite and provoke.

Ksawery Pruszy´nski, a great Polish journalist, wrote:

> A journalist must always feel responsible. He must take into account the effects which his writing will bring—whether he will encourage people to disregard the danger of the situation, or vice versa. . . . A good actor can never be booed at, but a journalist who has never been booed at, who has never acted against the public opinion, is a bad journalist. . . .
>
> The task of the journalist is not only to play a continuous musical tune to comply with the easy moods of the public; his task is to voice what he has arrived at in his reasoning; regardless of whether his reasoning is supported or rejected by the authorities, the Church, masses, society, nation, public opinion, he must be convinced that he gives a right advice or warning, even if someone does not like it. And a journalist must voice this to the very end. In spite of and against others. . . . He must say what he must fulfill, must repeat it until the end, even when the situation is getting worse, when he is not listened to, and particularly when he is not listened to.

Otherwise, we will be like fish on the sand. . . .

Adam Michnik is editor in chief of Gazeta Wyborcza *in Warsaw, Poland. In the struggle against communism he co-founded KOR (Committee for the Defense of Workers) and was instrumental in the Solidarity movement. He has published books and articles worldwide. This essay was translated by Elzbieta Petrajtis.*

11

Breaking Censorship—Making Peace

Gábor Demszky

We all start life wanting to be autonomous and free persons, members of the order of free thinking that faces censorship the world over. Censorship is the most anachronistic thing in the world. If we look back at history, the censor is seen as a comical, even a despised figure.

New censors, however, appear day by day. They like to mask their activities as the defense of elevated values, the avoidance of unforeseen dangers and the ultimate protection of a brave new world. They refer to God, king or the homeland; always something sublime. They claim that it is for our common good that we not see, read and know everything we are interested in.

Censorship is not on the right or the left. It cuts political families in the middle. I have spent half of my life in a political system where secret policemen could easily walk into your apartment or read your diaries. If they thought that things they saw were not friendly enough for some kind of reason of state, the writings could have been confiscated, their authors imprisoned. In this system agents of the Communist Party decided which books were not to be published, which were harmful to the pure soul of the people. Even questions of literary criticism were decided by party decrees. Fortunately, that system now belongs to history.

On the other hand, while I write these lines the dismantling of communications satellite aerials is being ordered in Iran. Thus, law-abiding citizens in that country will not have a chance to learn any opinions other than the ones the state feels are right for them. And in

Serbia, desperate intellectuals demand that radio and TV transmitters be bombed by NATO planes. They claim that it was the ruthless instigation of state-censored media that prepared people for war and the same censored media are responsible for maintaining war psychosis.

When I joined with other Eastern European dissidents at the end of the '70s, I already knew that the existence of censorship increases the danger of war. Censorship makes counterarguments silent. Under censorship difference is portrayed as enmity; opponents are demonized. Censorship makes people stupid and fanatic. All this meant imminent danger for humankind where the intercontinental missiles of world powers, missiles capable of destroying the Earth, were arrayed against one another. In communist countries censorship was a totalitarian endeavor for limiting global communication. We Eastern European dissidents understood that obstruction of communication increases war danger. This is why we said: *Breaking censorship is making peace.*

We thought that it was making peace because it was yet another proof that no Iron Curtain can be built in front of ideas. But we produced not only ideas, but information as well. We published and uncovered infringements of law committed by communist governments. After this, authorities had to think twice if they wanted to continue. They could, but they did not feel any more that what they were doing was a secret. The first crack in the walls of the totalitarian system appears when citizens do not believe any more that their government can do whatever it wants to them and others.

Our goal was to break censorship and increase possibilities for freedom in our region. After 1956 and 1968 we also understood that freedom can only be increased in any Eastern European country if solidarity is also increased among the region's populace. Thus, it was the first activity of the Hungarian democratic opposition to issue a statement of solidarity with the imprisoned Czechoslovak spokesmen of Charter 77. Permanent contacts were also established between Czech and Hungarian members of the democratic opposition.

I can also mention my own example. The reason I could operate an underground publishing house for a decade in Hungary was that in the spring of 1981 I was taught, in Poland, how to publish homemade books and journals. After the Jaruzelski *coup* I had a chance to return the favor of my Polish friends. Leaders of the *coup* closed down the western borders of Poland and expelled foreign correspondents to stop uncensored news from leaving the country.

They never thought that information could reach the West via Budapest. Every morning, however, I had been waiting for the Bathory express train arriving from Warsaw. I took out messages placed in our mutually agreed hiding place and sent them directly to the Paris office of Solidarity.

We Eastern European dissidents practiced nonviolent opposition. Our goal was to increase possibilities of freedom, step by step. We knew that breaking censorship was a "minority sport." The majority generally could maintain its welfare between given limits of censorship. It is true, however, that members of the majority were not at all happy. A demon whispered into their ears the same sentence we had heard for years: Our biggest value is to maintain our spiritual freedom. For those who gave this up it is quite bitter to hear the demon again and again. We never believed that the several decades of brainwashing made for a "Homo Sovieticus" people who did not need freedom any more. We knew that if we broke new taboos day by day, this would help others make one more less-dangerous move to increase their own personal freedom.

As 1989 gave way to 1990, dictatorships collapsed, almost at the same time, across the whole region. It was not the indulgence of the Moscow Politburo any more but our own wisdom that made us realize our ideas of freedom.

Today, looking around as a former underground publisher, I can feel safe. My portable printing machine has become an object in a museum. The old totalitarian regime that sought complete control over information is no more. With it, classic censorship—which wanted power over the whole of culture, the totality of life—perished. I know that in liberal democracies there are power groups which sometimes use indirect forms of censorship. Yet in such democracies there is room for maneuvering between different centers of power. Pluralist democracies are not always ideal, but they cannot establish a total monopoly on discourse. And new media increase communications opportunities for those pushed to the margins of society. The kind of censorship that I knew under communism is not likely to return.

If I look around as a politician, as the mayor of the biggest capital in the region, I am more pessimistic. Citizens of Eastern Europe are long over the euphoria of breaking the Iron Curtain in Hungary, staging the "Velvet Revolution" in then-Czechoslovakia or the dismantling of the Wall in Berlin. In most countries in the region, basic institutions of open societies such as free press, independent jurisprudence and multiparty systems have been built with impressive speed. On the other hand, many have lost their sense of security. People look in surprise at an increase in crime. They gaze at pictures from the Bosnian war in horror. They listen to news about the horrifying gas attack against the Tokyo metro or the bombing in Oklahoma. There are many who think, "In communist times such things did not happen. It is the excess of freedom that led to all these horrors." They tend to forget that in communist times, not only cults but churches as well could not operate. That not only paramilitary groups were outside the law, but all groups that were not founded by the state.

I see that there is an increase in the numbers of those who were silent during the communist era, but who now enjoy delivering angry and patriotic speeches. The former cowards are now the loudest. They would like to punish openly those who collaborated in the old system—that is, everyone who reached a position higher than themselves in the old hierarchy.

These heroic latecomers do not draw their present political legitimacy from their previous reputations, nor from their roles in the fight for democracy and freedom, but from their verbal patriotic feelings—from their nationalism. The essence of this is hate. They believe that the only proof of their deep patriotism is to show how much they hate foreigners.

Many in the West speak in disappointment about the new democracies in Eastern Europe. Ethnic conflicts stand behind this disappointment, mainly the war in the Balkans. It is true: What is happening in Bosnia is tragic and unacceptable. It is an outrage of civilization that the community of nations let things go this far. The war in the Balkans, however, is not proof of the fact that the nations of Eastern Europe could not live with possibilities offered by freedom after the collapse of communism. Just the opposite: The war shows where things end if communists stay in power. Unlike the leaders of one-party dictatorships who fell throughout Eastern Europe, Slobodan Milosevic of Serbia and his party stayed in power. The Yugoslavian republics were drawn into war by a communist elite.

Is a similar conflict in another country of liberated Eastern Europe possible? Perhaps. But in those countries where democratic opposition was strong before the collapse of the communist system, right-wing nationalist movements are relatively powerless. In Hungary, for instance, extremist parties could not win any seats in Parliament. In the former Czechoslovakia, the operations of democratic dissidents were virtually limited to the Czech part of the country; such activists were a rarity in Slovakia. After the separation of the country, right-wing nationalists did not have an important role in Czech political life. The same cannot be said of Slovakia.

In recent years, however, we have awakened to the realization that the collapse of state rule does not automatically provoke the triumph of democratic arrangements in all spheres of life. We must develop and adopt new rules of conduct. Tens of millions must unlearn ingrained habits and archaic reflexes. We are collectively enrolled in a vast "Democracy 101" course in Eastern Europe. The role of the press in this is inestimable.

Nevertheless, we learn all too frequently about how politicians in some formerly communist nations attempt to gag newspapers, radio or television. If not so brutally as their predecessors, they too attempt to curtail the freedom of the press. Direct censorship has vanished in the written press, but there are recurring attempts to undermine outspoken newspapers by crippling them economically. An equally pressing concern is that many Eastern Europe countries are reluctant to liberalize the establishment of radio and television stations, leaving the state monopoly on broadcast media virtually intact. He who fights for the freedom of the press in Eastern Europe today is more than likely engaged in a battle against state monopolies, since monopoly by definition implies inadequate freedom.

Under communism most people thought of the freedom of the press as a kind of luxury—a pleasure to have, but something they could do without. Since then, however, citizens have learned by experience that the autonomy of the media and the right to speak freely are not perquisites but guarantees of freedom. They are the very token of liberty, a liberty won so late and at such a dear price in this part of Europe that people will never surrender it again. Freedom has become one of our most cherished values. I take this as the safest guarantee of the demise of censorship, which is destined to become a phenomenon so irrelevant that in the future it will arouse only the interest of media historians.

Gábor Demszky, a sociologist, is the mayor of Budapest, Hungary. During the communist years he directed a samizdat *publishing house.*

12

A Tyranny of Images

Monroe E. Price

It is generally taken for granted that "independence" is a good thing for the press, that an independent press is necessary for democratic government, and that we know what we mean when we say a newspaper or television or radio station is "independent."

In the American view, independence for the press largely means immunity from government interference. But throughout the former Soviet Union, independence has come to mean not only independence from government, or independence from ancient theologies of reportage, or independence, even, from the influences of the West. In the emerging battle for identities in Ukraine or Kazakhstan, Estonia or Azerbaijan, independence has often meant, above all, freedom from televised images produced by Russia.

In a shakily independent Ukraine or Kazakhstan or Estonia in 1992 and after, a major question was autonomy from the imperial center, from the cultural forces that held sway for 70, if not for hundreds, of years. The monumental television transmitter in Moscow was symbolic of the process. A steel pylon with a huge concrete base, massive in proportion like the Egyptian pyramids, it represented the power to send a signal throughout the vast domain not only of Russia but, metaphorically, through the entire territories of the former Soviet Union. It epitomized the power of the desire to assert a monopoly over public thought. The transmitter became an encumbering remembrance of the past and an indication, through the signals it transmitted, of the complexities of defining the independence of the future.

81

In Kiev, for example, Russian, not Ukrainian, had predominated as the language of both the state and the media. Surprised at its independence, Ukraine had to determine what attention should be given to the cultural element of its identity. This was not only a question of changing street names, or of finding new purposes for the palatial but empty Lenin Museum. The very imagery of nationhood was to be forged.

Nevertheless, for an average household in the Ukraine, on an average evening in the early days of independence, the television set was turned to Moscow, to the glitz and professionalism of Ostankino, the First Channel, as opposed to the more amateurish, more unpracticed presenters at home. Moscow was the home of a post-Soviet teenage music culture, producing short videos with quick cuts, computer graphics and the look of the West. Lights flashed on and off, electronic effects cast their technological spell. Ukrainian folk songs and country dances could not compete. And the tendency of the young Parliament to demand time for its deliberations compounded the problem of fashioning a Ukrainian alternative to the Moscow diet.

In the remembered days of the USSR, Gostelradio had been the supreme voice of the state and the party. There had been no competition, and the stolid presentation had been a tribute to political and cultural monopoly. Television in the republics had been organized with some minor modicum of separateness, but the organization in Kiev had been subordinate to the administration in Moscow. The executives and the news presenters had all understood what it meant to be in a command society and what risks not to take. They had been charged, as well, with using the medium not to underscore divisive differences but to reinforce solidarity and the cultural and political superiority of the center—Moscow.

It was not only in the living rooms of Ukraine that one could see the consequences of these practices of cultural domination. In the offices of Ukrtelradio—the Ukrainian state radio and television monopoly—there was a virtual acknowledgment, in 1992, of the continued drawing power of Moscow television. The officials there had to compete with television from Moscow that had become miraculously younger and Westernized in the Gorbachev period. Programs had more razzle-dazzle; rock videos appeared together with culture and news. Anchors had brand name recognition. There were glamorous hosts and hostesses, fashionable and daring clothes and beguiling, softly erotic shots of 15-year-old rock stars. Moscow, in its new regional incarnation, had chosen to deal with the problem of which culture to carry by going global.

Moscow's transformations were important; they reverberated all over the old empire. At the beginning of 1992, with the decline of the Soviet Union, the First Channel, formerly the flagship for Gorbachev and for each leader before him, was in danger of abandonment. The enterprise, a centerpiece of the Soviet Union, now needed a client. Russia itself was the major candidate, but there was an intriguing alternative: an all-commonwealth channel, one dedicated to maintaining an informal sense of the region, with a voice that acknowledged the new sovereignties but remembered the old ties. Such a role might have been all the more important if the budget of the First Channel were to be dependent on specific allocations from each of the republics. And indeed, a Council of Presidents of all the republics initially considered such an arrangement.

But this view placed the newly sovereign nations, like Ukraine, in an unusual position. In the first year of their independence, Ukrainian officials were sensitive to every slight. Tested on all fronts as to their distinctiveness (from military to language policy), trying to appear separate and distinct, they believed that Moscow television was inflammatory, insulting and particularly biased on Ukraine-Russia relations. Daily news and interview shows were scanned for a pro-Russian, anti-Ukrainian perspective.

For the media czars in Kiev it was a matter of concern, if not embarrassment, that although they had obtained political severance from Russia, Russian television dominance still continued. Indeed, the ministers of the new Ukraine considered alternatives: pressing for the closure of the Moscow First Channel and the dividing of its assets, jamming its signal or imposing a governing structure—through the Council of Presidents—that would make the channel less biased, at least from the Ukrainian or non-Russian perspective.

Instead, there was a temporary but complex compromise. Ukraine and the other republics would no longer finance program production on the First Channel; Russia would pay the bill. On the other hand, Ukraine would not charge for the transmission of the signal to its country's inhabitants. The consequence was a curious, impermanent, and intermediate cultural imperialism—one that recognized historic links between the former Soviet republics and the substantial continuing Russian population in Ukraine and elsewhere. The force of this now-external Russian programming was so ingrained that no government, particularly at a time of economic deprivation, could risk the consequences of its elimination.

The struggle for "independence," then, assumed many forms—human, historical, geographical, financial. The formerly Moscow-controlled Ukranian state television sought a new future and a charter to find and promulgate a national identity that would support the new status quo. Its citadel in Kiev would be a large modern complex built in the last decade of the Soviet empire. Rather than consider the new edifice an inappropriate symbol for the press in a post-totalitarian state, the old bureaucrats of Ukraine dedicated this broadcasting city to a brave new world of statist broadcasting for Ukraine, where a new officialdom and a new national identity needed buttressing. Maybe architecture would be as good a guide to its future as the images that scurry across the reformed television screen.

Three years later, the question of imagery and geographical independence from Moscow was sharpened as the relations between Ukraine and Russia became momentarily more severe (as would be true between Russia and many of the former Republics). In spring 1994 the tense relations between Ukraine and the Russian Federation found a spark in disputes over Russian broadcasts thought to encourage a breakaway Crimea, and over the rights of Russian journalists—now called "foreign correspondents"—to accreditation in Kiev and Kharkov. Leonid Kravchuk, then president of Ukraine, had stated that coverage on Ostankino and in other Russian media was biased against Ukraine, and that it was weakening support for his state. Ostankino journalists working in Kharkov and Odessa were denied accreditation. Was this action retaliation for an ill-received slight, the start of a "media war" or something else? An adviser to the Ukrainian embassy in Moscow, Vadim Doganov, contended that the action was specific to these journalists and was because of their "nonobjective reporting." He claimed that the government acted in accordance with the new Ukrainian media law.

"Independent" broadcasting was emerging in Ukraine and elsewhere but it was not necessarily serving the goals which inspired its advocates. The central broadcasting empire had been weakened. That was certain. But it was far from evident that the gap had been filled with indigenous broadcasters independent of the state, using that independence to ferret out truth, to empower ordinary citizens in the democratic process and to provide access to means of self-expression. True, a generation of publishers, editors and journalists was training itself and being courted from abroad. True, the process of adaptation was proceeding full tilt. But as elsewhere in the world, the hoped-for commitment to more independent television news and public-service broadcasting was little in evidence in a society where an appetite for advertising and a new mood of deregulation were the call of the day.

Monroe E. Price, editor of the Post-Soviet Media Law and Policy Newsletter, is Danciger Professor of Law and director, Howards M. Squadron Program in Law, Media and Society at the Benjamin N. Cardozo School of Law at Yeshiva University. The article is adapted from his book, Television, the Public Sphere and National Identity, *published by Oxford University Press in 1995.*

13

Exporting American Media

John Maxwell Hamilton and George A. Krimsky

Since the rapid fall of communist dominoes five years ago, Western media experts, academics, foundation executives and government officials have filled up hotels and classrooms from "Stettin in the Baltic to Trieste in the Adriatic" and penetrated far behind what Winston Churchill once delineated as the Iron Curtain.

This profusion of media foreign aid on such a scale is unprecedented. Not unprecedented is the attitude of these experts, mostly Americans, who bump into each other with the same journalism gospel tucked under their arms: "Democracy is impossible without a free and commercially viable media."

The very scale of these advisory efforts can be reassuring. With so many experienced people trying to achieve the same result, how wrong can these Americans possibly be?

But such self-confidence may not always be justified. It is still too early to know how effective all our media assistance will turn out to be. But it is not too late to ask what is realistically possible, or even desirable, in transforming press systems abroad.

American journalists have long had a passion for exporting their media system. During World War II and its aftermath, journalists pressed the U.S. government to support free-press initiatives abroad. One reason was self-interest. News organizations wanted to gather news without interference from foreign governments. Another was the betterment of the world, which Americans frequently did not distinguish sharply from their own news-gathering objectives. The United States had the best press system, Kent Cooper, general manager of the Associated Press, said at the time; "it would be wonderful if the force that is available from that success would be directed altruistically...to the rest of the world."

These free-press missionaries could point to results on paper. Peace treaties with Italy and Germany required their new governments to promote press freedom. In 1945 the General Headquarters of Allied Occupation Forces in Japan promulgated a Press Code that called for objective reporting in that country and actually required journalists to separate opinion from truth and factual news. Journalists pressed the case in Latin America, and later in Africa, fostering academic and professional exchanges and training.

Some countries were more successful than others in developing a free press. American efforts to help were haphazard and limited—until the fall of the Berlin Wall in 1989. The prospect of stepping over the dilapidated Iron Curtain and taking the message of a free press all the way to once-closed cities like Vladivostok propelled journalists into action. They readily found partners. The International Media Fund, funded by $10 million from Congress, dispatched trainers and equipment throughout Eastern and Central Europe. The Independent Journalism Foundation, founded on a grant from the *New York Times,* set up training centers in Prague, Bratislava and Bucharest. The Eurasia Foundation provides small, quick-response media grants in the former Soviet Union. It is funded by the U.S. Agency for International Development (AID), which had previously left media matters to its poorer cousin, the United States Information Agency (USIA).

U.S. universities—Boston University, Columbia University, the University of Georgia, Indiana University, the University of Iowa, Louisiana State University, the University of Maryland, the University of Missouri and Rutgers University, to name a few—began training programs. New York University's Center for War, Peace and the News Media launched Russian-American Press and Information Centers in Moscow, St. Petersburg and elsewhere around Russia to provide a forum for exchanging information and ideas among indigenous journalists. The Freedom Forum, the German Marshall Fund of the United States and the John S. and James L. Knight Foundation began to make major investments in overseas programs primarily directed at former communist countries in Europe. So many planes were whisking journalism trainers to liberated lands in Europe that the Center for Foreign Journalists, the only full-fledged international media training institution that existed in the United States before 1989, set up a clearinghouse to keep track of who was doing what east of the Elbe.

The fall of communism justifies hope for democracy, but by itself the fall of the Iron Curtain does not mean the rise of a more independent press system. The more important question is, What kind of social, economic and cultural system exists in the wake of its departure? All of these factors are crucial in determining how a new press system will develop in these countries.

Perhaps no foreign-aid task is more difficult than fostering a free press. A truly independent press, in the financial and editorial sense, is more difficult to create than a market economy, because a self-supporting media system requires a free-market system as a precondition. Without the means to earn its own way through advertising and profit-making ventures, a press must be linked to special interests—such as a government, a party or a narrow business concern.

Attitude as well as economics hamper the development of a free press. As the Hutchins Commission on Freedom of the Press put it in the 1940s, "journalism is a profession grafted on to an industry." Thanks to their news traditions, however, American journalists have generally managed to isolate themselves from business considerations and created an extraordinary newsroom ethic that values objectivity and aggressive reporting over profits. This cannot be willed into being overnight. No one can mandate objective, balanced reporting. The concept is too slippery and penalties are impossible to impose if a media system is to be truly free.

Finally, an essential ingredient in independent journalism lies outside the media altogether. The success of the American system depends on readers who understand the role of the press and on newsmakers who know how to work effectively with free media to develop support for their own policies and programs. Appreciation of this comes only over time.

It is one thing to suggest that transforming a press system is difficult. The real question is what the transformation should lead to. The common view is that not only is the U.S. model of a privately owned, independent and fact-based press the best one for everyone; it is also the only one that works. But is it? Consider these three countries.

The Philippines has an open, civilian-governed democracy; it also has one of the most vibrant, colorful presses in the world. At any given time at least 15 dailies circulate in Manila. By U.S. standards, however, they are not reliable. Rich owners subsidize most newspapers, which provide a cacophony of views and gossip that is anything but dispassionate. Somehow, though, the people get the information they need to function in a democracy. Adlai Amor, a veteran Filipino journalist, says the key lies in the "multiplicity of voices." The readers are shrewd and skeptical enough to draw their own conclusions about motives and agendas in the news.

Lebanon has the strongest, most independent and most sophisticated press in the Arabic-speaking world. Its 3.5 million citizens have 20 newspapers. (Egypt, a country of 57 million, has ten.) But a press that is independent from the government doesn't automatically promote a functioning democracy. Thanks to the country's virtual civil war of the 1970s, which the media greatly contributed to, Lebanon is a mess politically, socially and economically. According to Lebanese journalist Tewfik Mishlawi, publisher and editor of the *Middle East Reporter* in Beirut, most of the country's national press aligned themselves in the 1970s with various political interests. The resulting war of words contributed to the civil violence that erupted in 1975 and is only now subsiding.

France is a well-functioning democracy whose press, unlike that of the United States, takes pride in being ideological and partisan. Its news columns are more like essays, and readers are loyal to a particular point of view in their favorite newspaper.

Such views are unusual among U.S. journalists, but they predominate around the world. South African Rich Mokhondo, with Reuters in Johannesburg, wisely notes, "objectivity wasn't enough" to correct social ills in his country under white rule. It should not be surprising that at this stage of development in newly independent countries, many journalists prefer to tell readers what to think. As many a Russian editor has said, "We've been deprived of our opinion for 70 years, and nobody is going to keep us from speaking our minds now."

Americans are often uncomfortable with such approaches to the news business. But the issue is not what Americans prefer or believe works well in their own country. Rather it is what the recipient is willing to do and what the recipient thinks will work. The question for those who provide foreign assistance is how to help newly independent countries construct their own systems.

The most basic form of foreign aid is tangible resources, either money or equipment or bricks and mortar. Unfortunately, this is difficult in media assistance.

As in any aid effort, what the recipient wants and the donor is willing to give are not always compatible. Eastern and Central European media managers frequently request financing or donations of equipment such as computer hardware, software and newsprint. But they may bridle at American offers of a new philosophical rationale for their press system. "Stop talking about an 'intellectual Marshall Plan' from the country of McDonald's and shopping malls," a former Yugoslav journalist angrily told a conference at Columbia University in 1992. "Give us your software and leave us alone."

While many Westerners do agree that tangible help is needed, it is neither easy to provide nor always desirable. American businesses are not keen on making investments because they consider media in these countries to be a bad risk. Although investors from industrialized European countries have been more willing to make investments, this is not an ideal solution from the point of view of struggling media companies in newly independent countries. Such enterprises, which fear that they will have to cede some control to investors, prefer outright grants.

Foreign-assistance dollars from American government agencies and foundations present problems too. Donors either can't or don't want to pay big bills for equipment and facilities, such as nongovernment printing plants. They don't want to become bogged down in the never-ending subsidy business, such as replenishing newsprint supplies (which are both pricey and in near-constant shortage). Because donors could never hope to fund all the news operations that have sprung up in newly independent countries, they would have to choose among them, a role they should not presume. Finally, foreign aid from the American government necessarily involves the government of the recipient country, which typically oversees its use. This makes the journalists beholden to government officials, precisely the outcome the West is trying to avoid.

A broader philosophical issue is also at work here. Capital transfer cannot compensate for an immature market economy, which has a small advertising and consumer base and massive distribution problems. If the ultimate goal for the independent-minded media in these countries is economic self-sufficiency, a credible argument can be made that material assistance fosters continuing dependence.

This is not to say that equipment donations are hopeless, especially if done on a modest scale. The International Media Fund and USAID's Eurasia Foundation have effectively managed equipment donations by carefully selecting their recipients and filling precise, immediate needs. Usually these infusions of money have filled a crucial void in a newspaper or broadcast station's production or distribution process, such as a typyesetting machine or small radio transmitter. The Freedom Forum has also been effective in creating and donating complete media libraries, replete with computerized access to global databases. But generally speaking, material assistance is not the panacea.

So what does all this say about the concept of media assistance? Should Americans give up and let others muddle along? Or does the United States have something substantive to offer?

The answer is that Americans can offer a great deal in the more amorphous but badly needed area of know-how, which in foreign aid terms is called technical assistance.

The new generation of reporters and editors in newly independent countries have benefited from a strong and universal education system. But they have had little exposure to fact-based journalism and none about how to survive in a competitive environment without subsidies. Anyone who has listened to Russian journalists say that they do not like "goal-setting" because it sounds too much like the old communist approach understands how difficult it is to unlearn communism.

The American media system is made up of many component parts. Trial and error and a vast array of "needs assessments" have shown that virtually all the components have appeal to one overseas group or another. In some cases there is interest in learning to balance editorial costs and advertising revenues, and in techniques for increasing circulation and advertising. Others benefit from ideas on meeting community needs with reliable, local news. Still others are interested in specialized reporting on the environment, or business or investigative journalism. All are strengths of the U.S. system.

Literally hundreds of workshops, seminars, conferences, and one-on-one coaching sessions have been held over the past five years, both in the United States and abroad. The dictates of time and money have for the most part limited this assistance to fairly brief durations. The most successful programs have concentrated on limited, concrete goals.

Given the goal of self-sufficiency, one yardstick for measuring the contribution of technical assistance is what has been left behind. Although some may leave the tangible legacy of a how-to manual tailored to local conditions or a course curriculum for journalism educators, it is impossible to measure the ultimate success of technical assistance with any precision. Few trainers can point to anything as dramatic as a doubling of circulation after a workshop. When Patti McCracken of *U.S. News & World Report* went to Slovakia as a Knight International Press Fellow, she considered it a great victory when she convinced the news staff at a Bratislava weekly to sit down for the first time with the graphics staff. Such small advances in "process" produce results that may only become apparent years later, and in ways that the experts might not have predicted.

Central to such effective technical assistance is the idea of helping, not directing. One American who was teaching Pacific Island reporters how to pursue feature stories went along on an interview with the local police chief and ended up in a shouting match with him over accusations of police brutality. What should have been an arm's-length relationship with the reportorial process became a counterproductive eyeball-to-eyeball confrontation.

The technical assistance that works best is the technical assistance that is the least presumptuous, that offers recipients the greatest opportunity to explore the portion of the American system that seems most relevant to their situation, and that then lets them adopt methods that fit local conditions. The Center for Foreign Journalists, which administers the Knight Foundation's fellowship program, gives new fellows this advice: "You are going abroad to share the tools, not build the house."

In the United States, journalism training occurred *after* the rise of a free and autonomous press. Journalism schools were created to instill concepts, like objectivity, that already had taken shape in newsrooms, and which owners realized enhanced the market value of their news product. Providing technical assistance in newly independent countries puts training ahead of, or at least parallel with, the building of a market economy. If there is an element of risk in such an approach, it nonetheless appears that it offers the most potential for creating an appreciation and awareness of the possibilities of an independent-minded media system.

Americans have a tradition of imbuing foreign policy with deeply felt moralistic sentiment. This is particularly true in foreign aid, and the result is disastrous. When a foreign country pursues its own course, rather than follow the American model, Americans feel that aid recipients have not just rejected U.S. advice but spurned Americans themselves. Advocates of a free press risk this same problem. They must realize that the burden of change is not on them, but on the recipient. And that in the development of a strong media system, it is less important that those being helped adopt the American system entirely than that they create their own. Independence, in the final analysis, requires the freedom to reject American imperatives.

To take any other view is to ignore our own heritage. The United States media system, like the United States economic system, evolved slowly. Initially it was tied to special interests, highly partisan and often irresponsible.

Technical assistance offers the best vehicle for nurturing the development of a free press abroad. But any endorsement of this approach must include *caveats.*

First, we must continue to work at making technical assistance culturally sensitive. This requires some experimentation. As participants at a recent Washington conference on media assistance suggested, of possible interest are programs that train trainers to carry on after the foreign experts leave. We must face the fact that we are only beginning to learn how to help.

Second, it is a mistake to concentrate media assistance only on journalists. If the media are to be part of a larger system of open, democratic government, then the whole system must be developed. Many government officials have no experience developing public support for change and must learn techniques for working effectively through an independent media. If these leaders do not feel that they can work effectively through a free media, they are more likely to revert back to old authoritarian approaches, which threaten all their reforms.

Third is the matter of geographic imbalance: Technical assistance needs to be made extensively available in other regions of the world. We do not think that too many people are in Eastern and Central Europe and the former Soviet Union. In fact, more could be usefully sent. The demand for technical assistance far outstrips the supply, especially if one considers the clumping of experts in the capital cities.

But democratic possibilities and independent media systems are struggling to emerge around the world, not just in white, European countries. In Latin America democratic variants have appeared in Brazil, Paraguay, Argentina, Peru and Nicaragua. At about the same time the world first heard the word *glasnost,* a form of it was being experienced in such African countries as Ethiopia, Zambia, Tanzania, Mozambique, Namibia and even Nigeria, Zaire and Rwanda. But they received little attention or assistance and now face the prospect of getting less. Americans have spent an estimated $25 million in media assistance in Eastern and Central Europe and the former Soviet Union from 1990 to 1995, about four times as much as has been spent in the rest of the world over the same time period. No wonder the Nigerian ambassador to the United Nations declared that "the Cold War is over and Africa lost."

Foreign media assistance requires a long-term view. Patience, not a quick fix, will make the difference. There is time for return trips by teams that with each visit become progressively more savvy about local conditions. Americans must spread assistance over many years as well as many countries.

And they must go abroad with an understanding that freedom, democracy and true independence are created by peoples, not handed to them.

John Maxwell Hamilton is dean of the Manship School of Mass Communication at Louisiana State University.

George A. Krimsky, an executive training consultant, is former president of the Center for Foreign Journalists.

III

Journalism as a
Democratic Discipline

14

Regaining Dignity

Robert MacNeil

It is still strange to me that standard usage lumps such bewildering variety under a singular term, *media,* not only because it offends linguistically—what is the plural of media?—but because it may be responsible for some of our problems with the public.

Ten years ago I quoted Daniel Schorr as saying "the words 'power of the press' always carried a white hat connotation of power exercised for good. But 'power of the media' has a black hat sound of power exercised against people."

And there is no question that the news media have problems of credibility and trust. That was the burden of my remarks ten years ago and the signs are worse now. I am square enough to think that all this still matters. I will argue that it matters fundamentally, and I will argue that it does not matter a damn, and you can choose which you find more convincing.

Why should elements as diverse as those that comprise our media of communications, information and entertainment be considered *it?* Even narrowing the field to news media, how can we encompass the *New York Times* and "Hard Copy," C-Span and the *National Enquirer, Foreign Affairs* and "A Current Affair" in a single term? Surely the name *media* inappropriately besmirches some as it launders others. The term *media* now engenders such contempt in some quarters that to apply it to all our journalism institutions is like calling all hotels flophouses.

Obviously it's futile to complain. The usage is fixed, but the more we call media *it,* the more the public will think so, the more our own minds will be confused about what we should be doing, in particular how much to borrow from the seductive entertainment media. It is time to think a little more singularly, discriminatingly, about *our* identity as journalists.

Unfortunately we can't just take our section, the news media, in isolation. The developments of the past ten years show that compartments between this and other segments of the media are not colorfast. Our products are tossed in the same frenzied laundromat of competition for the public's attention and dollar, and the fabrics bleed into one another. The ravishing colors of entertainment media bleed into the necessary black, white and gray of journalism, both literally and metaphorically, in print and video. Advertising, public relations, politics, religion, education, popular arts and science are all washed together these days. The result is often a coat of many colors, tie-dyed in the eyes of consumers, who, especially the young, could probably care less about what category of media they are consuming.

The range of media activities now resembles the electro-magnetic spectrum. All human activities, from a Mozart opera to pornography, to war on Saddam Hussein, to a learned article in a scientific journal, to a movie like *Pulp Fiction,* to a presidential news conference, to a chronicle of the Civil War, to the computer on which I composed this talk, are reducible to digital bits and bytes, ever more tightly compressed, ever more quickly flashed in mega-, giga-, tera-, or exa-byte quantities around the globe in the blink of an eye, like the billions in currencies traded in milliseconds in transactions more powerful than the power of great nations.

When it's all reduced to the abstract language of computers, it is human nature, especially human *business* nature, to think of it all as "stuff" to be sold, pushing the stuff that sells best—books, operas, sitcoms, magazines in print or video or TV—jettisoning what does not sell, whatever its artistic or public service value to a few. Classical music does not sell as hugely as popular music, so in one of the world capitals of music, New York City, another FM station converts to pop and we are left with two sources for classical music out of dozens for pop.

I do not worry about the business world. It has always taken care of itself and has often led other needs in advancing communications.

Moneymaking, like love, will find a way to communicate.

I think we should worry about *our* side, the journalism part of the spectrum, because that is where the mental stability of this democracy partly resides. Unless the keepers of journalism guard their values, it will not merely be market share, ratings, circulation that suffer; it will be a further erosion of the fundamental understandings of this political culture. Just as we are on the verge of another huge leap into the unknown—the total internationalization of news information—my biggest concern is this: How well are the astonishing leaps in media development serving the democracy and its institutions? Are we making miracles with our dazzling exploitations but *un*making in the process the best miracle man has yet invented for human happiness, the modern democratic state?

About ten years ago our known media universe exploded with a big bang and everything flew into fragments that have since been coalescing into new galaxies: the old and new television networks, satellite and cable companies, movie and publishing empires, record companies and video rental chains, home shopping and telephone companies, all still colliding and merging, or shattering and reconverging differently. We are probably still at too young a stage in the birth of this new media universe to know which will come to rest as fixed stars and which will burn out, but the heavens are still trembling at their nativity, shareholders and employees from shock, and more detached observers from anxiety about what the new constellations will mean.

There's an analogy with print magazines. The breakup of big nationals spawned thousands of special-interest magazines. The wider spectrum means more choice for splinter segments of the market who can gravitate to their own interests.

Ten years ago, before cable television discovered the catnip of courtroom drama, O.J. Simpson junkies would have been forced to watch a network summary every night. Now they can get the trial from other sources, live on CNN and Court TV. The *New York Times* reports that this is driving network nightly news ratings down by some 10 percent, because some people would rather continue watching the trial live than go to the summary on a network program.

In other words, viewers are choosing to make their own synthesis, watching news in the rough or wholesale, e.g. on C-Span, or more *à la carte.* I wonder how many people in the future will want the synthesis recognized news organizations offer and how many will want to make their own. Cy Simms may have it wrong for us: An educated consumer may be our worst customer.

The really sophisticated and moderately prosperous information consumer can right now, through his computer, bring in just about any kind of news he wants from anywhere in the world. If he wants to invest in a satellite dish, a cable service and access to the Internet, he can snatch just what he needs in financial and business news, sports, entertainment and politics, from any publication, any news program, any library—and flick Bill Clinton or Newt Gingrich a little E-mail zinger into the bargain. He doesn't have to wait for an electronic newspaper, or hypertext. He can dip into any newspaper, and he can order a pizza, book an airline flight and buy a sweater from J. Crew all at the same time. Of course he has to be a little nerdy to bother, but in the age of Bill Gates nerds are cool.

Ten years ago I found it worrying that journalists were feeling growing competition from uses of the same media where facts were something to be played with, manipulated, improved, even ignored, to make a better docudrama, movie, play, pop song, commercial, political speech or sermon. In a media context where fact and fiction co-exist so intimately, I worried that it must produce in some minds a blurring of the distinction, perhaps an indifference to the distinction, perhaps a contempt for the real facts.

Now, fast forward through the decade that has seen Oliver Stone's movie *JFK*; NBC rigging a GM truck gas tank to make it explode; CBS whispering assurance to Newt Gingrich's mother that no one else would hear her indiscretions about Hillary Clinton; ABC showing as news footage a re-enacted spy scene; the videotape marketed by Jerry Falwell retailing the wildest rumors about the Clintons as the established truth; the enormous popularity of crime and syndicated news shows which deal in facts fictionally recreated; the sudden growth of talk radio where paranoid opinion may replace facts; and the wholesale borrowing of supermarket tabloid standards by mainstream media in the O.J. Simpson orgy.

Some of those practices were widely criticized and apologized for by the three network news departments, because they were considered breaches of journalistic standards the nation had come to trust, standards the networks stoutly reaffirmed. But huge chunks of the population, and the democratic electorate, are no longer bothering with the networks. Their share of the nation's attention, once roughly 90 percent at suppertime, had fallen to 77 percent by 1980, 58 percent by last year, and is currently (with the O.J. Simpson trial deficit) at less than 52 percent.

To go back to the Roper survey, that means millions of Americans who used to get information from institutions with respected journalistic credentials are now getting it from talk shows that grow ever more lurid and leering, real life crime and rescue shows, syndicated tabloid news, docudramas and re-enactments—where traditional journalistic standards seem irrelevant. And Roper says that half of Americans find these programs "fairly credible sources of information," striking a particular chord with people often described as alienated from the Washington-Wall Street axis—the poor, the less educated, the young and the old.

So, increased competition in the marketplace may be the enemy of conventional standards of journalism. The question is whether these hot new kinds of information programming, with their high entertainment values and appeal to the young, are forcing serious journalists to follow them for survival.

And the O.J. Simpson story is evidence that they do. Simpson swamped the networks. Certainly, Simpson was a great story, touching all the American obsessions with sports, celebrities, lifestyles of the rich, domestic violence, interracial marriage and sex—perhaps a modern Othello but in a racially inflammable society, with his own lawyers ironically doing their best to inflame the issue.

In addition, there was the spectacle of a man rich enough to spin a legal web that would take a year to unravel, a process that for an ordinary man would be a matter of weeks. And it offered legal and media personalities an opportunity to preen and posture on an astonishing scale. All the world's a stage in the Simpson case. Kato Kaelin was a celebrity guest, along with Bill Clinton, at the annual dinner of the Radio-Television Correspondents in Washington in 1995.

On many nights the networks led with O.J. When they did, it said to half the population in the world's leading democracy that these respectable sources of responsible information considered the latest O.J. Simpson twist the most important thing that happened in the world that day. Of course the network journalists didn't think that, but they feel competitively obliged to put Simpson first to get customers into the tent. Ten, 20 years ago they would not have.

It illustrates an alarming trend in which the bottom-feeding media appear to drive even the serious big fish to make everything more entertaining.

Well, I promised to argue that all this doesn't matter, so here goes:

First, if Americans hate the media but love their favorite paper or TV show, why does their abstract hatred matter? Anyway, the same cognitive dissonance applies to Congress, schools and other institutions.

The media reflect the temper of the times. They do not create that temper, although they may shape it, crystallize it, magnify it, make it more extreme and raise its pitch.

If there were a *real* threat to the nation, Americans would snap out of this mood and get serious. The crisis would stimulate and focus their energy behind a common purpose. The Gulf War—certainly a tenuous threat to this nation—showed that.

In other words the marketplace, which often supplies such prurient and voyeuristic drivel now, will solve the problem. The media will get serious when they see the country getting serious, when they see the audience for serious stuff out-rating the audience for circuses.

But we have just seen what solutions the market is providing, and now I want to argue that it *does* matter.

The evidence I have given is one-sided, stressing the negative. (Dear me! How unfair!) We all know there is plenty of sound journalism and reliable information—if you want it and know where to look for it. All true. I'm in the business and I can't keep up with all the good material there is to read. To *read:* There's the rub! There is much less that tempts me to watch, and *watching,* not reading, is how most Americans get their information and have for three decades.

If the trends I have discussed above continue, the information presented to them will increasingly be driven by entertainment choices, not journalistic. I think we are on the edge of that mattering a great deal.

One can speculate about what effect it will have on a nation already more polarized socially and economically than in the past, and polarized in terms of civic responsibility. No other democracy has such a large percentage of alienated or indifferent voters, people who feel that the exercise of choosing the country's leaders is irrelevant to them.

As information viewing turns more tabloid, will these Americans be helped to reason or understand their self-interest? Hard to say.

Will video literacy increase the worldliness and intellectual discernment of the democratic electorate or weaken it? Does it reduce the skepticism that reading inculcates? Is it making Americans more credulous? Who knows?

But as Gore Vidal has said, for a millennium the word has been reason's only mold. How will the new literacy mold our reason? People spend far more of their time with or at television than the masses ever did with print.

Even with all the limitations we've talked about, television connects them with the country and the world on a more sophisticated level than generations ago. But *not compared with one generation ago,* when the three networks' prestigious news departments had a monopoly on the nation's attention, and their nightly news programs had a dignity and seriousness that would make even the "MacNeil/ Lehrer NewsHour" look glitzy. The question is the quality of the information and how its presentation shapes the mind, memory and reasoning powers.

The essential thing in a democratic society is to bring the average person into play as an informed participant. It is important to bridge the gap between the elite who will always know and the others who seldom know. I think it was true in the past, say from the Second World War to 1980, when popular as well as serious journalism shared common assumptions that made the nation one.

That is where the new questions point: Are the media trends we've been discussing helping to de-alienate, un-confuse, make a more useful citizen of the average person? If that average person has increasing contempt for news media, where will he get the information on which to base his role in the democracy? Are we contributing to his anger, his bitterness, his disenchantment with the institutions of the democracy?

How far will this swing to entertainment drag serious journalism with it? Are we fated in the liberal democracies to degenerate into silliness—the British obsessed with their randy future king, we with O.J. Simpson? Or is this decadence temporary because society lacks any organizing, defining crisis or point to it all? Are we merely suffering from the terrible absence of the Cold War?

I don't know the answers to these questions but I wouldn't pose them if I didn't believe they are serious questions.

We have to remember, as journalists, that we may be trained observers but we are not totally disinterested observers. We are not so-cial engineers, but each one of us has a stake in the health of this democracy. Democracy and the social contract that makes it work are held tight together by a delicate web of trust, and all of us in journal-ism hold edges of the web. We are not just amused bystanders, watch-ing the idiots screw it up.

I have one practical answer, which is where I began. Let us stop thinking of ourselves as *the media,* just another of the rings in the circus, which the government and public can kick around. Let us kick the sawdust off our feet and take back some dignity. Let us take back the name of journalist. Let's try and rescue some young journalists before they all run away with the media circus, or join the cult of infotainment and are beyond deprogramming.

Names are important. We are what we call ourselves. And for 40 years I have been proud to call myself a journalist. I think media stinks!

Robert MacNeil is former executive editor and co-anchor of the "MacNeil/Lehrer NewsHour" on PBS. His essay is adapted from a speech delivered at the Media Studies Center's 10th anniversary con-ference in 1995.

15

Images that Injure

Brian Mulroney

Freedom is indivisible. You can't have prosperity without a free market or free speech. And you can't have either without a free press. Political assassinations and economic calamities and dramatic developments abroad actually have surprisingly little destabilizing effect on life in a great democracy. Whereas other more fragile nations are thrown into complete tailspins by such tragic developments, in many nations of the world our democratic traditions are so strong, and important public policy institutions so transparent, that life goes on with hardly a change. And in our nations—Canada, the United States and others—much of this powerful democratic underpinning reposes on the remarkable achievements of a free and an unfettered press. Our countries have made great and impressive strides. Perfection in this area, however, has easily eluded our grasp, even after more than 300 years of trying.

And so, we must protect our freedoms with our lives because our democracies will wither without a free press. The media has important rights and privileges in our societies, but they also have assumed vital obligations and responsibilities. The media must focus daily on the need to maintain balance and fairness and perspective.

Like most of us, they don't always succeed. There are some great and impressive media outlets in all of our democracies, thank God. But no one who has endured the malice of an incorrigibly hostile media will doubt the proposition that public service entails great personal costs for participants and their families. No leader who has seen responsible public policy initiatives subverted or smothered by mountains of trivia and drivel and trash will disagree with the notion that perseverance in the face of indignity is one of the fundamental requirements of modern leadership.

That said, if it is true that it is better for a guilty man to go free than an innocent one to be convicted—and it certainly is—it's also true that such personal abuse by the media has, to some significant degree, become an unfortunately high but necessary price for leaders to pay for the privilege of service in truly democratic societies. For example, in the 1992 primaries, then-Governor Clinton took more hits than the Bismarck, some accurate and important, but many that were false and contrived. When he persevered and won, the media announced—he had character. And yet had he faltered and lost, because of the same charges, the same Bill Clinton would have been castigated for life and pilloried in death as a loser—the most humiliating epithet an American public figure has to endure.

But the accusations against him wouldn't have become more accurate or relevant with the passage of time. A falsehood about a public figure loses none of its venom and gains no credence simply because it appears in print less frequently or prominently than it once did. Reflect for a minute on the words of former Labor Secretary Raymond Donovan, who, when he was fully exonerated of all charges brought against him in this city years ago, looked at the media and asked, "What door should I knock on now, to get my reputation back?"

I ask you to remember those words because politicians are not the only ones tracked these days by a certain media, or individuals masquerading as journalists. Politicians are only the most numerous, the most visible and, strange to say, often the most defenseless.

The fact is that political leaders who protest serious inaccuracy or bias are often dismissed as thin-skinned, or worse, someone with a "hair-trigger temper." Both, as we know, in the minds of the media, are grave and insuperable impediments to the pursuit of higher office. And political leaders who sue for libel and defamation frequently wind up ridiculed or broke or both—unless you're from Singapore! As they say in polite society, it just isn't done.

I preach for no parish any longer. I did that for a decade. I was prime minister of a great country for nine years and I was privileged to win two back-to-back majority governments. And while I was there, I executed, as best I could, the responsibilities of my office. And I have no complaints about the manner in which I was treated—today! But my only message today is the need for responsibility and accountability by the media, as they fulfill their indispensable roles as vigorous critics and faithful chroniclers of our lives and our times, our great failings and our high achievements.

And what inspiration would the media have for this? The American media? Well, I think that you could do no better than apply to your profession the words of Judge Learned Hand, the greatest American jurist who was never appointed to your Supreme Court, who, over 50 years ago, was down here welcoming immigrants to the United States of America—Jews and Irish and Catholics and Protestants and Muslims from all over the world.

And he was explaining to them what he thought was important about your society. And he talked about the spirit of liberty. And he said to immigrants that "the spirit of liberty is the spirit that is not too sure that it is right; the spirit of liberty seeks to understand the minds of other men and other women. The spirit of liberty weighs their interests alongside its own, without bias. The spirit of liberty knows that not even a sparrow falls to earth unheeded. And the spirit of liberty is the spirit of Him who, near two thousand years ago, taught mankind a lesson that it has never quite learned and never quite forgotten—that there may be a kingdom where the least shall be heard and considered side-by-side with the greatest."

That, to me, is a magnificent definition of the splendor of the American republic. That is the reason for your success: the respect for the spirit of liberty. And I believe that of American media and Canadian media which, by and large, have followed in a manner respectful of that great tradition.

If they continue to do what Judge Learned Hand advised, I believe that the North American media, in spite of difficulties, will emerge and continue to grow as a positive and dynamic force for good in our societies.

Brian Mulroney, prime minister of Canada from 1984 until 1993, is a trustee of The Freedom Forum and was formerly on the Media Studies Center's National Advisory Committee. He is a senior partner at the Montreal law firm of Ogilvy Renault. His essay is adapted from a speech delivered at the Center's 10th anniversary conference.

16

Scoping Out Habermas

Victor Navasky

Before I became its publisher, I used to joke that the secret of *The Nation*'s survival as America's oldest weekly magazine—we were founded in 1865 by abolitionists and their sympathizers—is that it lost money for virtually every one of its 130 years. As Carey McWilliams, who edited *The Nation* from 1955 through 1975 once noted, "It is precisely because *The Nation*'s backers cared more about what it stood for than what it earned that the magazine has survived where countless other publications, many with circulations in the millions, have gone under."

As it happens, in the United States the idea that journals of opinion, whatever their politics, are too important to be abandoned to the vicissitudes of free market economics goes all the way back to the first Congress, when politicians of all camps decided to maintain the preferential postal rates for newspapers (which in those days were journals of opinion) that Benjamin Franklin had established as postmaster. George Washington himself thought that they should be delivered free.

To these early citizens, schooled on such distinguished examples of printed argument as the pamphleteer Tom Paine's eloquent appeals to reason, and those more sober models of public discourse, *The Federalist Papers*, the contribution of opinion journals to the democratic conversation was perhaps self-evident. Inhabitants of this age of enlightenment saw themselves as members of a republic of letters where debate was the best defense against despotism.

By way of contrast, the citizen on the brink of the 21st century, besieged by proliferating cable channels, talk-back talk radio, the Internet and all manner of and opportunity for interactive communication and hyperactive debate, might well ask the question: Are journals of opinion relics of the 18th century? Are they really necessary?

No matter that TV is tabloidized, the mainstream press is Murdochized and far too much of the information produced by the megaconglomerates that dominate the new media landscape is commercialized, bureaucratized and homogenized. The received wisdom seems to be that the handwriting is on the wall for these stapled artifacts of the print culture, that these hold-outs for rigorous policy debate, the power of reason and the importance of moral argument, are literally outmoded.

But are they? Or has the market, by creating a press which incessantly appropriates, consumes, recycles and too often flattens ideas, turned over something of a monopoly in the business of dealing with serious ideas to the shrinking band of small-circulation periodicals whose heritage is to test, contest and fight for ideas, and occasionally even to put new ones on the agenda?

After 16 years of editing such a journal, last year I took a sabbatical dedicated to reading, thinking and writing about such questions and quickly discovered that these magazines already had an unlikely Boswell in philosopher Jürgen Habermas, whom I had previously regarded as indecipherable—both because of his jargon-ridden translated-from-the-German prose and his historic connection to the Frankfurt School, the first bastion of critical theory, which I found indecipherable in its own right.

But Habermas had also invented the notion of the public sphere (which I put halfway between the political or governmental sphere and the private and personal sphere), and it turned out that he identified the journal of opinion as a sort of house organ to the public sphere. In 1962 he elaborated his theory in a study which he jauntily titled *The Structural Transformation of the Public Sphere: An Inquiry into a Category of Bourgeois Society*. It was not translated into English or published in this country until 1989, but its first half turned out to include an ambitious analytic history of the organic connection between these journals and opinion-formation in a democratic society.

Stripped bare, Habermas's theory, in the Enlightenment tradition, includes the idea that to flourish, democracy demands continuous conversation, open argumentation and debate. This happened (at least for white males) in the city-states of ancient Greece. It happened again, Habermas observes, in 16th-century Europe when the conditions of mercantile capitalism led to the coming together of private citizens to debate public issues in an open way (what he calls the "bourgeois public sphere"). He traces this development to the coffeehouses which grew out of the salons of court, but also to the periodical press which set the agenda of coffeehouse debate—especially in England, where censorship was minimal. By the beginning of the 18th century there were an estimated 3,000 coffeehouses in London alone. Unlike the earlier newsletters which had reported on the journeys of princes and foreign dignitaries, on balls and other news of and from the court, these new periodicals like Addison and Steele's *Tatler,* Defoe's *Review* and Swift's *Examiner* included essays and satires that criticized the Parliament and Crown. Because this criticism was carried out in public, it had something of a transforming effect on Parliament and helped to usher in an era of parliamentary democracy.

Habermas's theory had particular resonance for me. I was already persuaded by Christopher Lasch's essay, first published in this journal in the spring of 1990, bemoaning the transformation of American politics into a spectator sport since the great days of the Lincoln-Douglas debates. Perhaps because Lasch's list of virtues associated with participation in public debate ("judgment, prudence, eloquence, courage, self-reliance, common sense") reminds me of the Boy Scout oath, Habermas's historical survey and analysis seemed to take Lasch to a deeper level.

But I also made a more personal connection. Two minutes down the street from the old *Nation* offices at 333 Sixth Avenue and right next door to the old *Village Voice* offices, where Christopher Street meets Sheridan Square, stands the closest thing to a 20th-century version of an 18th-century coffeehouse—the Lion's Head tavern. It is known for the political graffiti in its bathroom, its rare cheeseburgers and the overheated political and literary arguments of its denizens, many of whose book jackets festoon its walls. I spent far too many hours there engaged in (ahem) public discourse, but from Habermas I learned that I was carrying on an honorable tradition: In 18th-century London, Button's Coffee House contained a lion's head, and readers threw letters through its jaws. From then on, they were published weekly as the "Roaring of the Lion." So Habermas had provided me with both a philosophical analysis of my calling and a reminder of one of my hangouts. We had much to discuss.

I wrote Habermas and made him an offer: If he would answer my questions (either in writing or on a tape which I offered to supply), I would arrange for transcription and translation, share his answers with a seminar of my colleagues, type and transcribe their responses and share that with him. Not quite the face-to-face interaction we might have had at Button's, and not E-mail either, but not bad for a beginning. Habermas declined the honor. He was traveling, he was overextended, he had no time to compose answers, he didn't like to talk into tape recorders, and he didn't trust journalists, especially American ones. Then fortune smiled. I was invited to deliver a paper at the Louisiana Museum in Copenhagen and I accepted on condition that the round-trip ticket include a stopover in Frankfurt. I called his office to see if he could spare half an hour. Lucky for me, Habermas was on the road but his secretary wasn't, and she booked me in for the day before my talk in Copenhagen. By way of preparation I consulted various texts, including a transcript of a conference hosted by the University of North Carolina on the occasion of the English translation of *Transformation,* and since I was spending that part of my sabbatical at Harvard, I tracked down Prof. Seyla Benhabib, who had worked with Habermas. I found that she had useful insights into his distinct ideas about public life. Benhabib saw Habermas's notion of the public sphere as being informed by his democratic socialist values.

I was in the midst of packing when the phone rang. It was Habermas himself. There must be a mistake, he explained. He couldn't possibly spare the time, he was otherwise occupied and even if he weren't, the last American journalists who had passed through had betrayed him. He hoped that in all other respects my stopover in Frankfurt would be a productive one. When I told him that there were no other respects and asked if perhaps we could have an informal conversation, he relented—"but just for half an hour."

In the hour and a half I eventually spent with Habermas, in his spare two-room suite in a rundown gray university structure populated by cigarette-puffing students, he made a number of Habermassian points. Among them, when I asked what he thought about Lasch's lament for the institutions associated with public debate, he said "Breakfast." Say what? "Breakfast," he said, "is a critical institution, by which I mean that the reading of the morning paper at breakfast—and remember, *Die Zeit* and other European papers are closer in text to what Americans mean by the journal of opinion—gives you more time to consider rational argument. The morning paper is embedded with deep-seated cultural attitudes calling for time and attention—the scarcest of resources."

The role of the journal of opinion in the public sphere may have been critical in the past, but where does it fit in the information age? What did Habermas have to say about prophesies that electronic data banks will replace magazines and books and relegate them to a bygone age of print? Habermas described himself as old-fashioned in the sense that he believes in texts rather than oral presentations. He said he thinks that print (which he quaintly calls "the Gutenberg medium") provides certain healthy restraints on the processes of the mind. As a result, Habermas said, "the print media are still at the core of any media we have now." So much for the infobahn. He argued, in fact, that print media are the primary source from which TV and movies draw their substance. "A world without print—imagine it," he said. "The level of articulation and analysis would be left to drown. Print is a necessary source for maintaining the public sphere."

Do left- and right-wing journals play the same role *vis-à-vis* the public sphere, or do they have fundamentally different missions? "The left," he said, "is endowed with the capacity to feel nervous, it feels an obligation to provide innovative answers. Conservatives feel they already have the answers, which are to be found in tradition." Without minimizing the differences, he advised me "not to moralize them."

When I asked whether he thinks we may be in the middle of a paradigm shift that perhaps accounts for the civil wars within the various ideological camps, he said, "To use the label of 'paradigm shift' makes it too easy. Remember that paradigm shifts are discovered only after they come about."

But when I asked how he felt about the idea of objectivity — because many radical theorists applaud opinion journalism on the postmodernist ground that facts are constructs, meanings are indeterminate and objectivity impossible—he remarked that "Objectivity is the wrong question. What's important is extending the range of arguments. It's less important to what conclusion the writer comes. It is the auditorium (the audience) who decides. That is the critical thing." Granting all the *caveats* about the impossibility of objectivity, he added, shaking his head from side to side, "you should never drop the ideal of reliable information—if you do, everything is lost. Which is not to say that reliability is enough. In our business the requirements are beyond reliability. What is required is the highest level of discourse. You should try to follow the maxim to collect the best arguments for the most precisely stated position on the issue under discussion."

And then I asked the question that had brought me to Frankfurt: What is, what *should* be, the role of the journal of critical opinion in the next period? Although it may seem trivial or obvious when set down in black and white in the, er, Gutenberg medium, let me assure you that as it emerged in our conversation, it had all the clarity of the Liberty Bell. For anyone who entertains expectations of the public sphere, he said, these journals become extremely important. "At the core of their mission is to maintain the discursive character of public communication. Who else, if not this type of press, is going to set the standards?"

Who else, indeed. And there you have it. Listen to the man: "The key thing from the democratic standpoint is a critical audience which says yes or no. But now the question is how to keep the audience informed, how to keep it critical, how to keep it attending, how to keep it investing energy and so on and so on." In Habermassian terms all of these important functions should be fulfilled by the actors in the public sphere. "And in this division of labor those who are responsible for the journal of opinion—readers as well as writers and editors—should maintain that certain level of discourse."

This argument puts the importance of the journal of opinion in a new light. The conventional case for these publications has to do with the belief that their influence is far greater than their circulation. "No student of American society and its power relationships," wrote Hendrik Hertzberg in this journal in 1989, "would dispute that *The Nation* (circ. 80,000) is somehow more important than *Self* (circ. 1,200,000), *National Review* (circ. 150,000) more important than *Golf* (circ. 912,000) and *The New Republic* (circ. 96,000) more important than *Weight Watchers* (circ. 950,000)." His point: That these journals—through advocacy, analysis, interpretation and investigation—advance a project, tendencies and ideologies, and gain their outsized influence from the high quotient of opinion-shaping elites among their readers. In fact, it is asserted that if there is a limit on their influence, it is that "they preach to the choir."

Yet by putting the contemporary case for these journals in terms of the force of their arguments rather than the quality of their audience, Habermas (who elsewhere has observed that every subscription list is a political organization), has exposed as irrelevant the objection that opinion magazines preach only to the converted. But his message about how the contemporary mission of these periodicals transcends their traditional image as ideological proponents has particular resonance for the present moment.

For example, last year *The Nation* on the liberal left, but also *National Review* on the conservative right, each erupted in internal debate over U.S. policy towards Bosnia—whether to lift the arms embargo and bomb the Bosnian Serbs. In *The Nation* it was the human rights activists vs. the noninterventionists. In *National Review* it was the hawks vs. the isolationists. The values underlying each debate were poles apart—at *The Nation* they were informed by a humanistic internationalism, at *National Review* by what seemed to me a xenophobic nationalism. But civil war had broken out within rather than between the camps. And the issues ranged far beyond the Balkans. Where once there was consensus now there was argument, rethinking and even, Habermas to the contrary notwithstanding, talk of a paradigm shift.

It is, in other words, a time of apparent political incoherence. To put it another way, it is a time for journals of opinion to provide their readers with a coherent framework for analyzing, interpreting and debating the confusing issues posed by the post-Cold War political culture. In *The Nation*'s case, we aim at least for the evolution of a coherent philosophy, a new synthesis.

Meanwhile, the media pages of the mainstream press drown in reports of an unprecedented wave of mergers and acquisitions among leading publishing, broadcasting, telephone, computer, cable, entertainment and information companies. Billions of dollars change hands in multimedia deals. I can't, of course, speak to what this means for *National Review,* although it's difficult to resist speculating on how William F. Buckley Jr., its founder, reconciles his annual direct-mail appeals for funds with the journal's hard-line defense of free-market economics. But without calling for a return to the good old days of Addison and Steele's *Spectator,* when the production and consumption of opinion was the exclusive province of a white male gentry, I can say that one non-free marketeer left Frankfurt feeling that the paradoxes facing and surrounding the contemporary journal of opinion are less real than apparent, and that the mission of these particular Gutenberg entities was never more critical.

Victory Navasky, a 1994–95 Media Studies Center senior fellow, is publisher and editorial director of The Nation.

17

Public Journalism— Defining a Democratic Art

Davis Merritt

"How can you think and hit at the same time?"
—*Yogi Berra*

Baseball player Yogi Berra rejected any notions of contemplation while a fastball was on its way to the plate. Reflex took over—a trained reflex, but a reflex nevertheless. For journalists, the fastball is on its way to the plate every minute and hour and day; usually there's little time to work out complex rationales and delicate balances; just rely on reflexes—take a look, and swing.

It seems almost perverse. Journalism is an important democratic art. In today's geographically dispersed and increasingly inward-looking society, only journalism can provide the shared information and the place for discussing it that are essential to the democratic process. At its best, it creates the agora where democracy is practiced. But journalism must often be performed reflexively, under severe restrictions of time and space. And that practicality requires that its practitioners be "powerfully conditioned to its rules and values," as social researcher Daniel Yankelovich has put it.

In a very real way, the operational reflexes of journalism have become its culture—a culture so pervasive that it can be identified as One Journalism: the concept that there is and must be one homologous way of thinking and acting, guided by immutable and arcane rules.

Some of its traits include: the elevation of conflict, episodic coverage, an adversarial (as opposed to skeptical) stance toward all institutions, and the defensive use of the First Amendment to block any and all attacks. These have hardened into cultural traits that determine the way journalists frame stories and thus the way Americans receive their view of public life.

Public journalism seeks to define and learn a different set of reflexes, one that has a purpose beyond telling the news. It seeks to break away from the concept of One Journalism, with its idea that the rules and conventions of the profession are pervasive and inflexible.

One Journalism was fostered by the growth and concentration of media conglomerates, newspaper chains and broadcast networks over the past 40 years. The career ladders that concentration created meant that the journalism of New York and Wichita, Kan., and Washington and Spokane, Wash., became one cohesive set of ideas and ideals, one collection of fungible people and practices, its shape and tone determined by what happened at the top of the pyramid, not by the needs of any specific place or time.

Foremost among the reflexes fostered by One Journalism is an overriding philosophical reflex: detachment. Scholars argue about the origins of the tendency to see detachment as a virtue. Some contend it arose in the elevation of science in the 18th century, when the distanced observer came to be seen as the most reliable observer. Others say it was a later invention of publishers intent upon not appearing to favor one political or business faction over another. Whatever its origins, in this century the idea of detachment has hardened into a journalistic trait.

Detachment is widely believed to be the fount of our credibility. (This belief, I will argue later, is false.) Detachment as a guiding trait shapes the lens through which the journalist views the world and thus determines the view that the journalist projects. When one's job is defined as merely reflecting events, without regard for the broader consequences, when the role is limited to relating what experts and absolutists have to say on matters of public interest, citizens are defined out of the discussion.

The problem of the detached journalist is closely related to the problem of the transient journalist. One Journalism encourages a model of careerism centered on mobility that defines success as moving on and failure as staying in a place. It makes transience a virtue, but the effect of transience on the content and tone of newspapers and news-casts has been inevitably negative.

Transience chills passions about place. The allure of better jobs at larger places means that the journalist has no lasting stake in the community. The problems in the current town need not be resolved, only reported.

Historically, journalists have had a bit of gypsy in them, harking back to the time when printers with "a shirttail full of type" migrated across the continent looking for opportunity. But for reporters, an explosion of job opportunities in the middle of this century made transience a part of the job description. In the decade of 1971 to 1981, for instance, jobs in journalism increased 61 percent, birthing battalions of journalistic shock troopers who were anxious to make their careers. They had little concern for how their work affected life in one place because they would soon be in another. Detachment became part of the job description.

In the '70s and '80s an annual turnover of 15 to 25 percent in newspaper staffs was not unusual. Television's turnover, tied to numbers reflecting even small differences in stations' market size, was even higher.

Failure to move in two or three years was equated with career stagnation. Even at the level of top executives, the steamrolling expansion of chains and the network ladder created demand at newly acquired "properties." And as one link in the chain moved, others inexorably followed. With only some 1,700 daily newspapers in the United States, in a decade or less, changes in the editorship of even a relatively small number of dailies would affect a large percentage of newspapers and their communities.

The mobility driven by corporate expansion simply mirrored the restiveness of business and society. But increased mobility for journalists had a more pronounced effect on democratic deliberation than does mobility in most other professions, because a departing journalist takes away the potential for a long-term community view and an understanding of local knowledge and history that are essential if democratic deliberations are to have perspective and substance.

One Journalism defines good journalism as the kind of journalism produced at the top of the corporate pyramids—the networks and the major national and regional newspapers. This means that journalists address the particular problems and needs of a community in an artificial journalistic context, created in and driven from other places.

But people practice democratic government in specific locations, in the municipalities and states where they seek to answer the question, "What shall we do?" through deliberation. That process requires shared information, a place or method for discussing the implications of that information and some common values—above all the value that democratic deliberation is the best way to express and experience public life, and that all citizens have a personal responsibility to take part in that process.

The reflexive, value-neutral techniques of One Journalism do not promote democratic deliberation. Rather, their skewed definitions of sources and issues systematically exclude people from democratic deliberation and generate much irrelevant information that does not advance that essential deliberation. One Journalism determines, for instance, that we define "balance" as "both sides" when in fact most issues have multiple sides. It insures the high value we put on conflict as the ultimate illuminator of political discussion. It makes it inevitable that the world we present one day seems disconnected from the world we present the next day. Meanwhile, the culture of detachment denies any journalistic concern or responsibility for what happens, if anything.

When citizens see reflected in newspapers and broadcasts a politics of polar extremes that excludes them, when the machinations of experts and absolutists seem beyond their reach, they withdraw into private concerns. They abandon public life. This is a direct threat to journalism, for if people are not involved in public life, they have no need for journalists.

Journalism's authority—its right to be attended to—is disappearing in a cloud of cynicism and loss of credibility brought on by the routine and detached way we go about our business. But public journalism offers a solution to this problem. At its core, public journalism suggests a close examination of the alleged overriding value of detachment and seeks to develop more useful journalistic reflexes. Its objective is to find ways for journalism to serve a purpose beyond—but not in place of—telling the news: the purpose of reinvigorating public life by re-engaging people in it.

This requires both a change in the perspective of journalists and a change in what they do. It means learning to report and write about public life beyond traditional politics; to write about political issues in ways that reflect the true array of choices; to report the very important news of civic life—including civic successes—that now occurs outside our pinched definition of news. This can only be done if journalists think of the people reached by their efforts not as an audience to be entertained or as spectators at an event, but as citizens capable of action.

This response to the decline in public life and journalism conflicts sharply with One Journalism's guiding axiom of detachment. A key tenet of public journalism is that the "line" of detachment defined by One Journalism is a false construct. Traditional journalists speak of "crossing the line" as if three questionable things were true: that a single line defines all possible points of moral, ethical and professional concerns; that every journalist understands precisely where that line lies; and that anything on one side of the line is "good journalism" and everything on the other side is something else.

Think of the line not as a boundary, but as a continuum that runs between two points. One point defines total detachment or non-involvement in what we cover. The other defines total involvement, as when William Randolph Hearst reportedly cabled his artist in Cuba, "You furnish the pictures, I'll furnish the war."

Journalists exploring public journalism accept the construct of a continuum and seek to operate somewhere beyond total detachment but short of total involvement. Precisely where their activity falls is determined by their consciences, their judgment and the needs of their communities. Public journalism is the antithesis of One Journalism.

Traditionalists, believing that journalism's credibility springs from its detachment, raise alarms about a potential loss of credibility. As with the notion of the line, that idea doesn't stand much scrutiny.

Think of a person who has credibility with you. That person shares with you some broad common values, some fundamental views of life, that are the foundation of credibility.

Traditional journalism insists that it is honest, intelligent, aware, reliable and trustworthy—but insists that it has no broad view of its purpose in life other than to accumulate facts that are relayed as news.

But in a world awash in facts and events, people pay us not merely for information, but for our opinion about the relative importance of things. They will trust us in this endeavor and attend to our opinions only if they believe our opinions are based on some broad, shared values.

Public journalism is openly based on broad values as: This should be a better place to live, and people should determine what that means by taking personal responsibility for what goes on around them. Public life, according to the values of public journalism, requires shared information and shared deliberation; people participate in answering democracy's fundamental question of "What shall we do?"

Public journalism opens the possibility that journalists can serve their communities in truly useful ways that go beyond telling the news. It also offers us a chance to regain our lost credibility.

Making public journalism work means developing new journalistic reflexes. It means understanding that framing issues at the extreme excludes most people and searching for ways to frame them more accurately and inclusively. It means challenging the assumption that conflict is the most useful and interesting narrative device. It means avoiding the trap of episodic storytelling by understanding and relating the true context of events and the multiple consequences of choices. It means having an interest in whether problems are solved through democratic deliberation.

For instance, a news staff setting out to deal with a problem in a community would traditionally set out to answer the basic five Ws and an H: the who, what, when, where, why and how of the problem. Public journalism seeks to define another set of five Ws and an H. For instance, what would be, in the broadest sense, a good outcome? What is the goal? What mechanisms—government, private and public—might come into being to help attack the problem? What capacities to deal with this problem are missing, and how can those capacities be built and maintained? Who needs to talk with whom (and about what) to resolve the problem? What core values stand in the way of resolution and how and where can they be discussed? Where, and by whom, are some aspects of the problem being dealt with successfully and why?

For public life to go well, for democracy to regain its balance and fulfill its promise—and for journalism to regain its right to be attended to—journalism must continue to tell the news—and then do more to revive public life. No one, this early in the life of public journalism, has a copyright on how to turn its philosophy into newsprint and broadcasts. That's what all the experimentation is about, and that's why it is essential.

Those of us who think this is an important idea seek to interest others in the search for a better understanding of the dual problems of public life and journalism. We encourage them to join the search for an effective response to those problems. Success in this venture can be judged only over time, and the measure of success is whether democracy fulfills its promise; whether some impression is made on long-standing problems; whether this becomes a better place to live.

Davis Merritt was editor and senior vice president of the Wichita (Kan.) Eagle when this was written. He is the author of Public Journalism and Public Life: Why Telling the News is Not Enough. *This was the first book-length treatment of public/civic journalism by one of its principal architects.*

18

Journalists and Democratic Memory

Donald W. Shriver Jr.

Journalists say that they write the first draft of history. Historians say that they draft definitive history by waiting decades before attempting to sift the evidence.

But I want to explore the proposal that both journalists and historians are obliged to *redraft* history in the interest of their mutual service to the building of democratic public culture. Their goal should be to remember the past with the fullness, accuracy and empathy that prevent people from stereotyping one another and thus perpetuating their mutual enmity. The ability to look back and "see ourselves as others see us" is important because in its absence, great evils can flow. Consider this episode from the former Yugoslavia. In summer of 1993, an ABC News reporter asked a Serbian soldier, "Why are you at war with Bosnian Muslims?" Answer: "Because of what they did to us at Kosovo." The battle of Kosovo was fought in 1389.

Americans tend to scoff at the power of such ancient grudges, but some of us laid aside our scoffing in the fall of 1992, when the celebratory sheen of the quincentennial of the Columbus landing was rubbed thin by the protests of Native Americans: "Columbus didn't 'discover' us;" they charged, "he *invaded* us!"

I know well-educated white Americans who resented this outcry, but from the standpoint of the moral demands of democratic public culture, the resentment was not well taken. G.H. Mead, the social psychologist, defined that moral demand when he said that democracy depends upon the ability of citizens, when they step into the voting booth, to take account of other people's interests besides their own. That is one reason why all of us—including journalists—need to join in the project of redrafting and relearning history. Our growing national and world pluralism means confrontation with clashing human memories of the past. Unless we work at understanding this clash, we will chain ourselves to old orthodox versions of history that fortify alienation and inhibit our common democratic obligation to resist stereotypes of "my people" and "you people."

Political kinship assumes shared memory—both in what gets remembered and how. Journalists, politicians, educators, and religious leaders all help to shape that memory. My interest below is in the journalistic side of this responsibility, and I offer three extended illustrations.

In a series of 1992 *New York Times* articles on residential segregation of the races in suburban Chicago, Isabel Wilkerson interviewed one white woman who said: "It's up to them [African Americans] to paddle their own canoe. Don't always think about the fact that they were slaves."

The remark has many a parallel. "Why do Jews always bring up the Holocaust?" "Must you Indians always have to focus on how whites treated you a hundred years ago?" Translated into Chicago suburban terms, the remark means: "Be like us, even in how you remember or forget the past, and we will let you into our neighborhood. Of course, even if we let you let you reside there, we will not let you into our *minds* as though 'you' were one of 'us.'" I can imagine no clearer death warrant for democracy than all the variations on this theme in American and world society, for this is a formula for building barriers against an inclusive human community.

Happily there are counter-themes, and journalists like Wilkerson compose some of them. In the fall of 1992, Jack Miles, formerly an editor with the *Los Angeles Times,* mourned the riots of the previous spring in an article for *The Atlantic Monthly*. Surveying the employment statistics for African Americans in the city, he reflected ruefully that "last hired, first fired" was still the rule for many of these residents of Los Angeles, who regularly see immigrant Mexicans replace them as gardeners in the suburbs. This country, said Miles, suffers still from "that old and still unpaid debt" acquired in 250 years of slavery. The damage to African Americans carries over in the lives of some even to this day. And even if the day comes when all have finally shaken loose from the prejudices that the word "black" still conjures up in the minds of many a neighbor, to ask African Americans to *forget* slavery is on a par with asking Irish Americans to forget St. Patrick. For our common democratic education, *no* American should forget slavery, that great historical contradiction to democracy in the very founding of our government.

One might as well ask Jews to forget the Holocaust or Serbs to forget Kosovo. How might the latter have remembered it without using it to fuel a new war with Muslims? How does any painful public memory get delivered from its potential for repeating old wars? Political leadership that takes responsibility for redrafting public accounts of the past is surely a first answer. A certain kind of journalism is another. Consider the two ways in which journalists, say in January 1996, might respond to the Martin Luther King national holiday. Twenty-eight years after his death, a large percentage of American citizens, including journalists, will have no personal memories of King's career. They could write about the Civil Rights Movement as though it is ancient history, hardly worth detailed recollection in a news column. But tell that to African Americans facing racial prejudice in suburban Chicago! They know that William Faulkner's adage is reason enough to keep remembering that the struggle towards a democratic culture is far from over in America: "The past is not dead and gone; it isn't even past." Awareness of this pervasive fact ought to shape a lot of reporting on the King holiday.

In sum, one of the great intellectual and moral responsibilities of journalists is to keep us all reminded that today's news grows out of yesterday's, perhaps even out of many thousands of yesterdays. In a remarkable little column in the *New York Times* two years ago, Karl Meyer traced the roots of the Yugoslav crisis, not only in Kosovo, but to conflicts between Catholics, Orthodox Christians and Muslims going back to the Middle Ages. My guess is that television audiences who viewed "Roots," "Holocaust" and "The Civil War" found themselves surprised at what they didn't know about slavery, anti-Semitism and that greatest of our wars, and at how currently *alive* much of it seemed. The past is alive because it is already a part of who we are and who our neighbors are. But we need reminding of that and public reminding is one legitimate task of journalism.

War is the most traumatic of human events. That is why "war will not let us forget it," as my war-veteran colleague Roger L. Shinn put it. How will we remember it? In many ways, depending on whether one's ancestors won or lost, suffered or benefited from its aftermath. Divergent memories of our own Civil War accounted for part of the fascination with Ken Burns' documentary series "The Civil War." In 1995, we commemorated the 50th anniversary of the end of World War II. At that time, the political leaders of Germany, Russia, Japan, France and the United States planned the May and August ceremonies. The press covered these events. How would it provide "background" by way of interpretation? On every side, combatants and their descendants remembered the suffering. On every side, people resented the injustices of the enemy. How would newspapers and television enable us to appreciate the meanings of those memories?

Public debates over World War II in 1985, 1991 and 1994 provide some instructive cautions. The first was a six-week series of events that went by the name "Bitburg Cemetery": Should President Reagan visit it in spite of the dramatic plea of Elie Wiesel and thousands of American Jews that "this is not your place, Mr. President"? Why not? Because the bodies of 49 SS troops were buried there.

Seldom in recent American journalism had a strictly ceremonial event been covered over so long a period, in such detail or in such a complex knot of history, morality and politics. Reagan actually did visit the cemetery, but in the meantime the American and German publics received a refresher course on their citizens' different memories of the war in Europe. If they read the daily papers, they learned: that the SS was that section of Hitler's armies that systematically murdered Jews and other "undesirables"; that those troops were in charge of the extermination camps; that a president who speaks (as Reagan did) of all the German dead of the war as equal "victims" of Nazism betrays an incapacity for moral distinctions; that neither Jews nor millions of other Americans tolerate that incapacity in their president; that time alone, even 40 years, does not heal the wounds of horror suffered by one's ancestors; that accurate public recollection of such horror is one vital bond of democratic politics; that mere ceremonies count in the life of political communities, for what gets publicly remembered constitutes what remains publicly important; and that, in some human conflicts, controversy over the meaning of an old, religious-sounding word—"forgiveness"—counts too, even though politicians and journalists have a lot of trouble explaining it.

Having followed the Bitburg event closely in the writings of numerous American journalists, I can testify that as a whole, they deserve high marks for their descriptions of the complex of rage, puzzlement, shouting and listening which seeped into American public consciousness. At the end of the event, columnist William Safire wrote an eloquent summary worth quoting as an example of the way in which the tasks of public leaders, historians and journalists are sometimes remarkably akin:

> Ronald Reagan, a month ago, had no real grasp of the moral priorities of the Holocaust or the fear of forgetfulness that prevents forgiveness. His journey of understanding . . . opened the minds of millions to the costs of reconciliation in a way no other process could have accomplished. In driving home the lessons of history, his incredible series of blunders turned out to be a blessing.

In seeking at first to sidestep the smoldering resentments, the President brought on a firestorm 40 years after a Holocaust, which in turn forced a forgetful world through a most necessary grief.

There are other "necessary griefs" which journalists and other public leaders may have to invite, if not force, their constituents to remember about World War II. In 1995, we had another opportunity to test our combined ability to "redraft" public memory of the end of the war with Japan. We witnessed a rehearsal for this event in the 1991 observance of the 50th anniversary of the Pearl Harbor attack. Once again we Americans "remembered Pearl Harbor," and once again Japanese countered: "Remember Hiroshima." According to almost every poll in 1991, the standoff between the two publics on this point was profound. A late-fall proposal to offer the United States an apology for Pearl Harbor stalled in the Japanese Diet on the day George Bush abruptly dismissed the idea that the United States should apologize for Hiroshima.

Historians in Japan and the United States are not fully agreed on whether the atomic bomb was necessary for ending the Pacific War. Journalists are not responsible for arbitrating this question, but they could help educate both national publics to the "iffiness" of lots of decisions in war. They can rehearse the argument from both countries' points of view, and they could introduce a bit of empirical sobriety into the impenetrably patriotic memories of the war in both nations. If the fall 1994 fracas at the Smithsonian Institution over a proposed exhibit about the dropping of the atomic bomb is any indication, Americans are ill-prepared for such sobriety. We have low tolerance for asking whether our national leaders could have acted more wisely and humanely in conducting the war. Historians do agree, for example, that whatever one concludes about the Hiroshima bomb, the one that killed 40,000 people in Nagasaki was quite unnecessary to end the Pacific War—not to speak of a final 1,000–plane raid on Tokyo on August 14. Democracy is slipping in America if we ever buy into the slogan, "Brave soldiers and their commanders can do no wrong." More philosophically, we endanger human moral consciousness itself if we believe "The past could not have been any different," or "In a war right and wrong are irrelevant."

Much wrong was perpetrated on both sides of the Pacific War, as John W. Dower has massively documented in his study, *War Without Mercy: Race and Power in the Pacific War.* If American or Japanese politicians are ever to offer apologies for what our ancestors did to each other in that tragic conflict, we both ought to focus on racism. As Dower persuasively demonstrates, both sides exploited it as an ideological weapon. The Japanese called Americans "demons," murdered Chinese and Filipino civilians by the hundred thousand and conducted medical experiments on Asian prisoners equal to any undertaken by Dr. Mengele at Auschwitz. Americans called the Japanese "monkeys," condoned any number of Japanese civilian deaths as just punishment for Pearl Harbor and assumed that every American citizen of Japanese ancestry ought to be put into the American version of concentration camps.

So both sides have a lot to confess about the sins of their ancestors in this war. If publics on either side succumb to forgetfulness about these things, then all their commitments to "never again" are in danger of erosion. Naturally, the politician, educator and journalist who recalls these unpleasant moral ambiguities in the history of any nation's wars will risk unpopularity. If they mean to contribute to the improvement of Japanese-American relations in the years ahead, however, they will take the risk. German-American relations still have their share of "smoldering resentments" which Bitburg ignited into flame, but one of the great symbolic events of that incident was the speech of President Richard von Weizsacker to his Bundestag on May 8, 1985, detailing in an unprecedented public way the crimes of the Nazi era. People around the world, journalists included, hailed that speech as air-clearing evidence of German commitment to genuine democracy.

Germans and others sent Weizsacker two million letters of congratulation.

Less hopeful for democracy, a lot of smolder still stirs, like a lava flow, under the surface of Japanese and American memories of the Pacific War. Someday, when leaders in either country begin to acknowledge the justice of resentments still alive in the other, journalists should give their words sustained and careful coverage. Such reporting is vital to the cause of peace between our countries.

Journalists should give plenty of exposure to the recent gestures of Japanese prime ministers toward apologies to their Asian neighbors for Japanese crimes in the war. And since positive reinforcement is the royal road to learning, Americans need reminding of what their government did between 1976 and 1990 to issue apology and modest reparation to the descendants of Japanese Americans unjustly interned during the war. Racism triumphed in that internment; democracy triumphed in that apology. Government proved that it can apologize for the sins of its predecessors, and the American public was reminded that there are many forms of patriotism besides, "My country, right or wrong." Democracy requires another patriotism: "When wrong, now or long ago, let my country's leaders say so."

Journalists can help us all learn to say so.

Donald W. Shriver Jr., a 1993–94 Media Studies Center senior fellow, is professor of social ethics and former president of Union Theological Seminary in New York. His most recent book, An Ethic for Enemies: Forgiveness in Politics, *supplied some of the material for this article.*

19

Diversity, Democracy and Niche Markets

Nancy Hicks Maynard

It began as an ordinary lunch between two colleagues in publishing—one black, one white—discussing their business. As recounted in a June 13, 1994, *Washington Post* article, all was going well until literary agent Marie Dutton Brown casually mentioned that her client, *Essence* magazine editor Susan Taylor, had sold 250,000 copies of her book of inspirational essays.

Her luncheon companion almost choked. Then he patiently pointed out that Brown must have miscalculated.

"It's not on any best-sellers list," he said.

Brown stood firm. Finally, her companion, the editor at a major New York publishing house asked, "Who's buying it?"

"Black people," was Brown's reply.

What the editor found out that day—but many black authors have known for some time—is that the best-sellers lists do not capture millions of sales generated by guerrilla marketing campaigns, waged on behalf of niche audiences. Black authors have perfected this sales channel at churches, fraternal meetings and conventions to give their books blockbuster sales, even if such status goes unrecognized in the world of traditional publishing. In doing so, they are using the sales technique of niche marketing, which is becoming ever more significant as new information technologies enable writers and authors to reach carefully targeted segments of the public. As the ability to reach discreet communities skyrockets, the mass audiences scatter.

For members of historic minority groups interested in seeing their portrayal and employment opportunities improve in publishing, especially newspapers, the trend represents both good news and big questions. Within the niche system, groups can sell more easily and directly to natural audiences. They can reinforce familiar images of themselves, without regard to the world at large. This is the really good news. What is not clear, though, is whether and how people in different niches can develop a sense of shared values that is at the core of our nation's form of governance.

For American minority groups, the rising importance of niche markets is partly the result of mass media's failure to capture the essence of their lives and partly the result of new technological possibilities.

For almost 30 years, a host of organizations led efforts to increase the number of newspaper professionals who were members of minority groups. The rationale has been that those who interpret America's story everyday should reflect the demographic makeup of our society. But in a nation that grows browner by the day, those who report and edit the news are still overwhelmingly white. Years of struggle have moved the minority newsroom census from about 4 percent in 1978 to just over 10 percent in 1994.

The ultimate goal of this employment effort has been to change the portrayal of people of color in the news. Many ethnic communities complained over the years that news stories characterized them as pathological fragments of human beings, less intelligent, hardworking, honest and wealthy than they are.

Integrated newsrooms and new portrayals promised to create three separate opportunities: employment for minority professionals; new business for print and broadcast media; and social cohesion by creating common cause among people from different backgrounds.

Professionally, newspaper desegregation efforts have created career opportunities for thousands of talented journalists who are members of minority groups and were locked out of the industry earlier. It began in the '60s, when black activists demanded that they tell their stories to journalists who were black. Immediately, a host of staffers who had wanted to be journalists but worked in other jobs were given battlefield commissions to cover urban and campus wars. But many of these careers did not survive the urban peace.

As a founding member of the board and first president of the Maynard Institute for Journalism Education, I helped train and place hundreds of journalists from minority groups at newspapers. They did make a difference in their communities. One Mexican American man, working in Oregon in the late 1970s, learned firsthand how state police were systematically and illegally searching all Hispanic-looking men, seeking to identify aliens without documents. The resulting series was responsible for a change in state law. Many other Institute graduates have since become editors and reporters at the nation's largest news organizations. Some have won honors for their work, including the Pulitzer Prize. A few have become publishers. Yet at the time these efforts began, the industry had a hard time justifying desegregation. Publishers knew they were providing professional opportunities to groups historically excluded from the business, but could not see a market benefit from their actions. They did not understand they were locked in a cultural war. In addition, the news industry did not trust minority journalists to interpret the community-at-large in a professional way. As a result, careers stalled and many experienced journalists of color left the industry

Economic necessity changed all of that, especially in the largest markets. The last two decades have seen major cities' minority populations explode. Despite high levels of poverty in some groups, the minority middle class continues to grow. Now, opportunities for minority journalists are exploding as well in the emerging world of niche markets to serve a growing, educated population too often ignored in traditional mass media. These positions exist within big media organizations as well as in small independent operations.

New York City, for example, now has seven black newspapers, including the venerable *Amsterdam News,* with its paid circulation of 31,000, according to the Audit Bureau of Circulation. Four of the seven papers are published in Brooklyn, including the *City Sun,* established in 1984, with a paid circulation of 52,600. The *New York Voice* in Flushing serves 90,000 paid subscribers. These publications represent both opportunities and new vitality for older institutions as part of an emerging niche trend.

The creators of minority media, who have long worked in print, have expanded into new media. Minority entrepreneurs such as Quincy Jones bought broadcast and cable properties. Opportunities are growing in cyberspace as well. Within the last few years LatinoNet and the African American Information Network have been established. Another, Net Noir, recently started up. In New York, so too has an electronic bulletin board called Asian Pan American Resource Net. Almost all services heavily feature arts and politics, and some offer shopping as well. The list is growing so long that McGraw-Hill developed a guide to Internet Web sites of interest to the black community.

These growing career opportunities speak to the economic possibilities of niche marketing as well.

In the late 1970s, many of us working to desegregate the news media tried to make an economic argument to those in power. Any look at demographic projections showed minority groups represented the only growing population for the mature newspaper industry. This became even more of an issue for large metropolitan newspapers, as white residents continued to move away from cities. Editors and publishers could not then see minority populations as targets of market opportunity. In fact, neither could advertisers. I learned this during the 10 years my late husband, Bob, and I owned and published the *Oakland* (Calif.) *Tribune.*

Oakland is a unique city in the United States in that its population has no racial majority. It is approximately 42 percent black, 38 percent white and about 10 percent each Asian and Hispanic. There is no zip code in the city inhabited exclusively by one race. It is the home of Nobel laureates, many famous writers, world-class dining and some of the poorest Californians. The greater metropolitan market the *Tribune* served was about 50 percent white, 33 percent black, 15 percent Asian and 12 percent Hispanic.

Mirroring this large community, just about half of *Tribune* readers were members of minority groups. Half of *Tribune* readers earned more than $50,000 a year. Some 60 percent had attended college. The majority owned homes, whose average price was $255,000. Seventy percent voted, the highest civic participation of any readership in the Bay Area. Economically, this was as attractive an audience as advertisers could want. But that fact did not immediately translate into advertising dollars.

To begin with, advertising buying patterns did not help our efforts. Suburban business migration has left Oakland with only one department store. Clearly, though, our readers had to shop somewhere. But because advertisers traditionally place ads in newspapers in cities where their stores are located, big cities without adequate retailing and with concentrated wealth and poverty find it impossible to attract advertising in proportion to the residents' buying power. Reluctance in the marketing community expanded exponentially when the ethnic makeup of our market and readership became clear. Ethnicity often blinded advertisers to the buying capacity of the *Tribune*'s readers, making them reluctant to take out ads in our paper. The consequent shortage of advertising economically undermined the *Tribune*.

In one incident, a research group specializing in national advertising noted the sale of pickup trucks among our readers and concluded that ours was a blue-collar audience. In fact, they were relatively affluent people who, like a growing number of Americans, were buying sports and utility vehicles to replace the station wagon as the family work horse. Our family, for example, traded our Lincoln Continental for a Toyota 4–Runner, which at that time was classified as a truck to skirt import quotas; my lawyer sold her Mercedes and bought a Jeep. But the research firm, fixed on the image of lower-middle-class minorities driving pickup trucks, missed an important market trend among families who were solidly middle class. Thanks to this error, our company and our advertisers lost a great business opportunity.

Many of these problems are disappearing in niched markets. Niche marketing takes away the need for sweeping generalizations about people based on great big numbers and no real facts. As the specialized publications and on-line services show, technology is making marketing more indifferent to color. Somehow, not having to fit every audience into a common web of attributes and understanding is helping marketers reach audiences with efficiency.

New information technologies and niche marketing promise to further enhance occupational and economic opportunities. Potential social impacts are less clear. This boon for the market may result in lousy social policy if it causes enclaves to dominate our political structure to the exclusion of a common national vision.

Throughout history, newspapers have functioned as social glue. Unlike other news media, newspapers bound together disparate pieces of a society to create common cause and concern. Nowhere was this more evident than in the segregated South of the 1950s. Newspaper articles and editorials were pivotal in helping end legal segregation in our country.

Will that role disappear in our new world of niched media? It need not, if we manage the future properly.

Right now, the various American communities are still working off the same base of information. In its 1993 survey, Simmons Market Research Bureau found 62 percent of white adults and 61 percent of blacks read a daily. Hispanic readership was measured at 43 percent. Asian readership was not recorded.

The margins, though, show how tenuous the hold of mass media news could be unless they undergo structural changes to hold onto their role of social glue in a technologically sophisticated, niched information environment.

Our first step probably has nothing to do with segmented audiences. Instead, it speaks to the need to sharpen our journalistic tools of accuracy and fairness to regain the trust of readers. We've lost the trust in a rush to sensationalize the news to hold onto the audience that is fracturing naturally. In the process, we've cheapened our image in the public's mind.

Next, news publishers will have to learn better the art of packaging a core of stories, which would share a common subject matter but would be written and presented differently according to their format and audience. Political trend stories, for example, could have a common thesis for all niches but explain implications for the target audience. Editors began to develop these skills in a rudimentary way when they created zoned editions and special sections, sometimes in Spanish. New digital platforms will make such projects fairly easy, requiring little if any additional processing of stories.

There already are successful examples of specially filtered, general news packages in the *Wall Street Journal* and on MTV news and the Christian Broadcasting Network (CBN). CBN uses broadcast network news packages for visuals but tailors them to its audience with anchor reads and voice overs. In this sense, its news programs function much as competitive newspapers did in cities earlier in our lives: Each had many common elements, but that is not what defined them. Story selection, play and writing style were the identifying characteristics. And they probably will be again in cyberspace, especially the torrent of information packaged mostly for minority groups.

Then, if we learn to "gross up" niches, we can again have the efficiency of mass-audience distribution. That is the promise of new information technology. In this case, the mass in communications would be found in a multitude of common information linkages, rather than a single fare.

If we can organize our reporting and marketing efforts along these lines, the multiple purposes and promises of diversity in the news industry will be more than fulfilled.

Nancy Hicks Maynard, a former senior vice president of the Freedom Forum, was a founding member of the Media Studies Center's National Advisory Committee and former co-owner of the Oakland Tribune. *She is currently directing a study of the economics of news.*

20

Journalists—Professionals in a Market Culture

Margaret T. Gordon

Increasing economic pressures are creating new tensions between what reporters and editors feel are their journalistic responsibilities and what they feel called upon to do as workers in market-driven news organizations. Many believe that the pressures for profits now are encroaching on editorial decisions in ways that erode the quality of journalism.

As former *Chicago Tribune* editor James D. Squires reminds us in *Read All About It: The Corporate Takeover of America's Newspapers,* the historical and overriding purpose of the American press has been to educate the public. Squires, who has passionately detailed the inner conflicts and compromises that resulted in his 1989 resignation as editor of the *Tribune,* laments that today business pressures have caused corporate executives to regard *news* as "information surrounding advertisements" and *readers* as "targets of advertising."

Many journalists were attracted to the profession by the ideals evident in the First Amendment, the successes of the muckrakers, and the triumphs of reporters and editors who prevailed during Watergate. Such journalists believe their job is to provide citizens with the information necessary for the survival of our democracy, to protect the masses from scurrilous and dangerous practices of greedy entrepreneurs, and to be watchdogs on guard against fraud, abuse and excesses of elected officials.

Pioneers in the field worked hard to transform journalism into a profession on a level with learned professions such as law and medicine. They called for graduate education and developed a code of ethics, professional associations and publications. But unlike the other professions, they never agreed to licensing procedures or a strong system of peer-performance monitoring; these are seen as infringements of the freedom of the press guaranteed by the First Amendment.

Throughout American journalism, there has never been a time when it was purely an altruistic enterprise. Owners and investors have a right to make money. But has it gone too far? Are the First Amendment and professional ideals now being endangered by the drive for increased profits?

The sustenance of modern news enterprises is advertising; advertising rates go up when circulation goes up and down when it comes down. Despite well-documented declines in recent years in readership and viewership, Squires, Leo Bogart, Ben Bagdikian and others tell us that in the recent decade corporate executives grew accustomed to profits of 15 to 20 percent and some earned 30, 40 and even 55 percent. Not surprisingly, they have exerted pressure to maintain these unusually high (for American businesses) profit levels, even during times when newspapers are not doing as well due to factors such as declines in advertising, increases in the price of newsprint and pressures to invest in new technologies. Some say that instead of maintaining quality and allowing profits to decline, media executives have felt pushed to maintain profits even if it meant quality suffered.

Resources devoted to the production of news dramatically declined in the late '80s from an average of 20 percent of revenues to 6 to 8 percent. At the same time, as the number of print outlets and broadcast channels increased, the competition for circulation figures and audience ratings also increased. Market research techniques were employed to ascertain more about what the public thought it wanted. More and more, marketers told journalists what would sell; and more and more, journalists sold the public new "news products."

Marketer-defined news products include a host of new items: capsules, indexes, and "malls"; shorter, less detailed stories that don't jump from one page to another; formulaic accounts of crime and violence; sensationalized, personalized political stories; staged or pseudo events; teasers; talk shows, opinion shows and infotainment. With very few exceptions, new news products generally don't include reports on day-to-day government accomplishments, extended discussions of complex policy issues or much good news.

An irony is that although the journalists feel they are pandering to public tastes, the public's declining confidence in the press suggests that it is not pleased with what it is getting from the journalists. Further, 71 percent of the public thinks the media actually get in the way of our nation solving its problems.

One thing the public doesn't like is what it sees as incessant negativism, much of it fed by the rampant cynicism of reporters toward government and government officials. If journalists are continually publicizing blunders, conflicts and scandals, and rarely (if ever) publicizing innovations, achievements or outstanding performances, it is not surprising that a self-fulfilling prophecy has taken place: The public has little trust in government. Ironically, the public *also* has little trust in the media.

Instead of practicing the type of journalism that drew them to the profession, many if not most journalists find themselves pressured to respond in ways they believe to be anti-professional. They say they are expected to produce stories that, because of insufficient time or resources, fail to meet the norms of the profession, including such basics as double-sourcing key facts. They are pushed to personalize and sensationalize. They say they resent being expected to insert "edge" or "attitude" into stories, especially when it seems to be nothing more than a cheap shot. They don't like having to hype violence or dumb down their discussions of important and complicated public policy issues such as health care reform. And they tire of the formulaic approaches to topics they feel deserve innovative, creative treatment. They live with constant fear of being duped by media consultants and spin doctors. As reporting staffs are downsized, the remaining journalists fear for their jobs and too often feel they resort to story ideas designed to attract certain market segments rather than because they are important or interesting. Easy news, cheap-to-report news and trivializing approaches overwhelm the complex, the time-consuming and, too often, the important.

A significant number of journalists are less and less proud of their own work, less likely to believe that what they are doing is important and more unable to ignore the public's low ratings of their honesty and ethical standards. The once-healthy skepticism prompted by the official lies of Vietnam and Watergate has turned into constant, caustic and casual cynicism of journalists toward both the officials they cover *and* the public.

In short, the constant and increasing pressures growing out of the economics of modern American journalism clash with editorial values. Once, competition between rival newspapers would spur both to higher levels of journalistic achievement. Now most newspapers have no competition in their communities. They still have to worry about profits, but the incentive to produce better editorial products has declined. A number of long-term observers of the profession—devotees as well as critics—feel little hope that the profit pressures will ever ease, especially as they contemplate the potential effects of on-line news for advertising revenues. They are concerned there may never again be significant reinvestment in quality journalism. They fear the economic situation won't allow journalists to take back control over content from the marketers.

Nonetheless—quietly and away from the biggest news markets—there are some small steps being taken that could over time make some difference. For example, several television stations are experimenting with "good news" segments and features on people who have been innovators in government. More than a dozen communities are now experimenting with "public" or "civic" journalism designed to encourage citizen involvement in defining and solving community problems, and not incidentally, to encourage the public to become more dependent on locally produced news. This approach also is market-driven, but it would seem to have some potential for encouraging community-oriented, if not quality, journalism. In another approach, over 30 reporters and editors in Seattle have each "adopted" a school, donating time each week to help children read, discuss and understand the news, with the long-term hope of producing more newspaper readers, another healthy outcome for our democracy.

More fundamental suggestions for change are being urged by some in the profession but resisted by others: Leo Bogart calls for the development of a national media policy; Robert MacNeil urges us to drop the undifferentiated term "media" and embrace the term "journalist" with its old connotations and expectations; Tom Patterson suggests we shorten election campaigns; and fellows at The Freedom Forum urge consideration of standards for quality journalism and support for on-going media criticism.

While it is not clear which remedy, or *set* of remedies, can reverse current trends and reinstate the public's trust in the news media, one thing is clear: The news media now are failing in their First Amendment responsibility to provide people with the information they need to be informed, participating citizens. Fewer people trust the media or the government, and many are simply detached from the political process altogether. Journalists think the public isn't interested in *important* news—as opposed to more titillating, scandalous entertainment news—but perhaps there has been no real test of that idea. Perhaps journalists simply haven't risen to the challenge of making the other, more important news interesting enough to compete successfully with the new news products. Perhaps the solution is to increase quality.

Journalists need to confront the causes and consequences of the processes that have commodified the news, and they need to be willing to monitor their peers. If they don't or won't, they risk the profession being reformed from the outside, perhaps irreparably. Already there is a major threat in the public's declining support for the First Amendment; John Seigenthaler, chairman of The Freedom Forum First Amendment Center at Vanderbilt University, says he fears that if the Amendment were brought to a vote for ratification now, it might not pass. Loss of a Constitutionally-protected free press would destroy not only the profession, but our form of democracy.

Margaret T. Gordon, a 1985 Media Studies Center Inaugural fellow and 1994–95 senior fellow, is professor and former dean at the Graduate School of Public Affairs of the University of Washington.

21

Scorned in an Era of
Triumphant Democracy

Andie Tucher and Dan Bischoff

The first time we really noticed the decline in journalists' status in this democracy was the night MTV threw an inaugural ball for Bill Clinton.

It helps to remember that the MTV ball was *the* ball that year not only because Michael Stipe, Don Henley and Boyz II Men were performing, but because the President-elect had made it very clear that he was going to show up and turn the event into a symbol of the passing of the torch of Democratic governance to a new generation. We were both perfectly comfortable at that time with the new media revolution. One of us had toiled as a speech writer in the Clinton campaign's War Room, which had perfected the populist alternative to being kicked around by the Big Feet of mainstream journalism, and the other was then political editor of the *Village Voice,* which may not be "new media" but is at least frequently incoherent.

We figured we'd see a lot of our friends in the Washington press corps there. Sure enough, several of them were clustered at the door, where they were being held up by two lithe, gum-popping blondes in miniskirts. One reporter we knew from a national paper was virtually slapping his White House press pass—as if it were the staff of Moses—on their heads, saying over and over, "But I cover him *every day.* It's what I *do.* Like, for a full-time job."

To which one of the young things replied, crushingly, "We don't care about that. We're MTV."

Journalists aren't necessarily in the truth business—that's why it's called the newspaper business—but still, that was undeniably a *very* cruel truth: They *don't* care, at least not about the supposedly special role journalists play in our democratic political system. In fact, most citizens don't care about the political system itself very much, certainly not as much as they care about being entertained, and they care less every passing year. As a consequence, the prestige of both politicians and journalists has yet to find its cellar.

Which is sort of counterintuitive to most reporters, who take their part as democracy's Fourth Estate very seriously and today see it on the verge of achieving unprecedented international stature. Some four dozen countries have joined the ranks of the world's democracies in the past five years, and virtually all of them have simultaneously admitted independent Western or Western-style media within their borders. There are so many newly literate Chinese newspaper readers, for example, that their sudden demand for newsprint has sent its price skyrocketing, helping to close down the *Houston Post*.

The global expansion of journalism is undeniable and comforting in the abstract for any working journalist. Most of them take pride in the commonplace assertion that it was really Western European TV broadcasts into Eastern Europe that finally undermined the legitimacy of communist totalitarianism.

Look anywhere in the world today and you will see journalism (and its companion, advertising) carrying all before them on Rupert Murdoch's Fox, Sumner Redstone's Viacom, or Ted Turner's Turner Broadcasting. One could be forgiven for assuming journalists would be riding a wave of international prestige.

Yet nothing could be further from the truth—particularly in the United States. The long decline in esteem for journalists from its high point in 1975 has not been slowed by minor events like the fall of the Wall and the spread of democracy around the world. According to a Gallup poll taken here last year, barely one-fifth of the public ranks print journalists as either "high" or "very high" in "honesty and ethical standards." That puts us below even business executives, leaving only the stony consolation of being more highly esteemed than ad people, Congress and car salesmen. And a *Los Angeles Times* poll conducted in March of 1993 showed that only 17 percent of the respondents thought the media overall were doing a "very good job"—down from 30 percent in 1985. Forty percent said they have less confidence in today's media than they did when they first started paying attention to current events.

Part of the reason for Americans' disgruntlement of late is rooted in the old one, that nasty tendency to blame the messenger. But for messengers who work as journalists the blame has a special flavor. While modern consumers of news are certainly more sophisticated than the tyrants of old who used to lop off the head of anyone who brought bad tidings, they still have some very clear ideas of what they expect the media to do, and they don't take kindly to any that fail to fulfill their expectations and desires. The public's cardinal *expectation* is that the press will be objective. The problem for journalists is that the public's cardinal *desire* is often something else entirely.

Objectivity is certainly an honorable idea, at least. It may not in fact be possible for journalists to put aside personal biases and preconceptions to hold to some pure standard of truth, but for a century and a half now objectivity has nonetheless been a defining ideal for our trade.

It clearly seemed a step forward for responsible journalism when the founders of the penny press chose to seek their support from willing buyers in the open marketplace rather than from the stalwarts, zealots, and nabobs of political parties with deep pockets and deeper grudges. It seemed a step forward when Adolph Ochs devoted his *New York Times* to news that "does not soil the breakfast cloth" rather than calling for the assassination of President McKinley, as William Randolph Hearst had the bad taste—or bad timing—to do shortly before Leon Czolgosz accomplished just that.

But while the public has been well trained these decades past to expect objective reporting, they don't necessarily like what objective reporting has to say.

People ask a lot of journalism. They want it to do more than merely recount the day's events; it must explain the workings of the world and fashion them into a narrative that makes sense of what often seems senseless. It must account for everything from why wars rage to why politicians lie to why Tony Bennett made a comeback.

But because these are matters that touch people's most intimate and passionate beliefs, any commentary on them runs the risk of afflicting people where they are most comfortable. People want explanations—

but they want explanations that confirm their general assumptions about the way the world works, reinforce the facts they already know and uphold the beliefs they cherish.

It doesn't always work that way.

Of course the press can be guilty of misjudgments and prone to feeding frenzies. Of course headlines can be skewed and reporting slanted. And, yes, journalists often deserve the choice array of epithets flung our way—from arrogant and elitist to insensitive and dumb. But it's also true that even the most factual reporting often wrings from its readers or viewers that most bitter of childhood wails: "You're not being *fair!"*

When the press reported, truthfully, that Ross Perot said the Republicans were planning to disrupt his daughter's wedding, Perot's supporters tended to see this revelation of their candidate's looniness as proof not of journalistic thoroughness but of reporters' malice. When the press pointed out, also truthfully, that O.J. Simpson's own lawyers had advanced mutually contradictory alibis for him—the crippling arthritis and the golf swings on the front lawn—Simpson's supporters saw that as evidence that the press would never let him have a fair trial.

In fact, some 70 percent of the respondents to that *Los Angeles Times* poll agreed with the statement that the media "give more coverage to stories that support their own point of view than to those that don't." Of course Americans will feel betrayed when they expect both the appearance of objectivity and reporting that does not challenge their own vision of the truth. The root of the rampant dissatisfaction with the "fairness" of the media may well stem from one fundamental misunderstanding: People seem to believe that the definition of objectivity is "agreement with me."

And not only are the media of the late 20th century faced with the problem of meeting impossible expectations—there are now literally millions of *different* impossible expectations we can fail to meet. What we have now in this nation is not a public; it is a great noisy swarm of competing publics. We are not having open discussion or argument in the public square; we are in the middle of a food fight.

America is a nation struggling to come to terms with an eye-popping diversity, a nation where citizens often define themselves—willingly or not—on the basis of race, gender, economic status, national origin, religion, activist ideal, sexual orientation, health, age or shared obsession. We have a business community preoccupied with protecting its profits and a political establishment obsessed with its own perpetuation. For all these Americans, passively entrusting to the invisible hand of the market the truths that define their very being is just too risky. For all these various publics, "agreement with me" is more than a theoretical construct; it is a matter of life and death.

But we can't blame all of the problem on our readers and viewers; some of the culprits show up in the mirror every morning. When people answer surveys about journalists nowadays, they don't think of dogged little Woodwards and Bernsteins gnawing patiently at the clay feet of Richard Nixon, but of degrading spectacles like the pack of news hounds slathering at the feet of O.J. Simpson's lawyers. And the tradition these folks are spreading is not the one lectured about in American J-schools. What has been steadily happening, ever since the face of Princess Di sold an American magazine in 1980, is a hollowing out of American mass journalism—with its origins in graphic crime reporting and political scandal mongering—in favor of more global and gossipy Anglo-Australian tabloid styles, which have an almost glandular obsession with sex, social position, show business and fantasies of celebrity. In the person of Rupert Murdoch at the *New York Post* and in the inescapable currents of a newly international media culture, American journalism met the forces of tabloidization that would exacerbate the worst tendencies of the United States press.

A survey of eight Western democracies conducted by the Times-Mirror Center for the People and the Press in 1994 hinted at an interesting relationship between this sort of tabloid journalism and skepticism about the civic role of the press. Britain, which counts more tabloids among its major news outlets than almost any other nation, is uniquely hostile to newspapers: fully 23 percent of Britons said the press *hurts* democracy rather than helping it, more than twice the figure for any other nation surveyed. What's more, only 49 percent of British respondents felt the press was good for democracy, well below the 79 percent of Americans who believed the press play an important role in the democratic process.

Yet this is precisely the flavor of journalism on which the "new democracies" are being nourished. Is it any wonder that, while most of the new nations that have claimed membership in the free world in the past five years have indeed held "free elections" and established legislatures or political parties that mimic those found in Western Europe or the United States, it is frequently difficult to look at them and see what Americans would call "democracy"?

But what has happened in almost all these countries is a definite cultural opening to commercial mass media which often take on the colors of British tabloid journalism. In nation after nation new magazines—and often local versions of trash pop American mags like *Playboy* or *Cosmopolitan*—have sprouted like mushrooms after a heavy rain. In Russia, for example, where the ponderous mainstays of the Soviet press are finally losing their readers and their influence *(Argumenty I Facty* has dropped from a circulation of 25 million in 1992 to just 4 million today, and both *Pravda* and *Izvestia* are struggling to survive), surveys show that ordinary Russians are reading and watching less news-related programming on TV in order to read tabloids and watch talk shows and soaps. The most successful independent publications in Russia today are screamers like *Scandale, Express Gazeta,* and *Chastnaya Zhizn (Private Life).*

Internationally, journalism is not so much the Fourth Estate of government as it is a division of the entertainment industry—and a decidedly minor division at that, somewhere between "Entertainment Tonight" and the mail room at MCA. Fledgling global media outfits like Rupert Murdoch's Star TV now beam Phil Donahue, Oprah Winfrey, reruns of classic '50s sitcoms and current Fox staples like "The Simpsons" into fancy dachas on the Black Sea and herdsmen's yurts on the Mongolian plain alike, bringing the ideology of consumption (with all its ironies and tunnel vision) to peoples who have only recently left behind a lead-colored socialism.

In badly divided countries like the former Soviet Union, where the culture and the political economy lie like freshly ploughed soil, these sorts of media can more readily communicate a reassuring stability and context than can traditional, hard-nosed American news, which only seems divisive. News about Michael Jackson, the plight of Siamese twins or diet tips evokes the circular passions that encourage sales and confirm the unvarying inconsequence of daily life. Even O.J. (that universal solvent of objectivity), with its soap-opera-like cycles and tempestuous subplots, succeeds in diverting us from the great spiritual crisis the Cold War has left in its wake.

Serious journalism, on the other hand, can only remind us of the ideological confusion and moral aimlessness that characterizes current world politics. Who needs that? We rest secure in the knowledge that the President wears boxers, not briefs, and we didn't learn that from the Big Feet of mainstream news.

If that's what it takes to sell newspapers, the next Gallup poll will leave the journalists providing consolation for the car salesmen.

Andie Tucher is editorial producer of the ABC News Twentieth Century Documentary Project. She is the author of Froth and Scum: Truth, Beauty, Goodness and the Axe Murder in America's First Mass Medium.

Dan Bischoff is managing editor of the European desk for WORLDBusiness.

IV

Democracy and New Media

22

The Electronic Republic

Lawrence K. Grossman

A new political system is taking shape in the United States. As we head into the 21st century, America is turning into an electronic republic, a democratic system that is vastly increasing the people's day-to-day influence on the decisions of state. New elements of direct democracy are being grafted on to our traditional representative form of government, transforming the nature of the political process and calling into question some of the fundamental assumptions about political life that have existed since the nation was formed more than two hundred years ago.

The irony is that while Americans feel increasingly powerless, cynical, and frustrated about government, the distance between the governed and those who govern is actually shrinking dramatically. Many more citizens are gaining a greater voice in the making of public policy than at any time since the direct democracy of the ancient Greek city-states some twenty-five hundred years ago. Populist measures such as term limits, balanced budget amendments, direct state primaries and caucuses, and expanding use of ballot initiatives and referenda reduce the discretion of elected officials, enable voters to pick their own presidential nominees, bypass legislatures, and even empower the people to make their own laws. Incessant public-opinion polling and increasingly sophisticated interactive telecommunications devices make government instantly aware of, and responsive to, popular will—some say, too responsive for the good of the nation. As the elect seek to respond to every twist and turn of the electorate's mood, the people at large are taking on a more direct role in government than the Founders ever intended.

This democratic political transformation is being propelled largely by two developments—the two-hundred-year-long march toward political equality for all citizens and the explosive growth of new telecommunications media, the remarkable convergence of television, telephone, satellites, cable and personal computers. This is the first generation of citizens who can see, hear, and judge their own political leaders simultaneously and instantaneously. It is also the first generation of political leaders who can address the entire population and receive instant feedback about what the people think and want. Interactive telecommunications increasingly give ordinary citizens immediate access to the major political decisions that affect their lives and property.

The emerging electronic republic will be a political hybrid. Citizens not only will be able to select those who govern them, as they always have, but increasingly they also will be able to participate directly in making the laws and policies by which they are governed. Through the use of increasingly sophisticated two-way digital broadband telecommunications networks, members of the public are gaining a seat of their own at the table of political power. Even as the public's impatience with government rises, the inexorable progress of democratization, together with remarkable advances in interactive telecommunications, are turning the people themselves into the new fourth branch of government. In the electronic republic, it will no longer be the press but the public that functions as the nation's powerful Fourth Estate, alongside the executive, the legislative and the judiciary.

The rise of the electronic republic, with its perhaps inevitable tendency to respond instantaneously to every ripple of public opinion, will undercut—if not fundamentally alter—some of our most cherished Constitutional protections against the potential excesses of majority impulses. These protections were put in place by the Founders, who were as wary of pure democracy as they were fearful of governmental authority. The Constitution sought not only to protect the people against the overreaching power of government but also to protect the new nation against the overreaching demands of ordinary people, especially the poor.

Telecommunications technology has reduced the traditional barriers of time and distance. In the same way it can also reduce the traditional Constitutional barriers of checks and balances and separation of powers, which James Madison thought the very size and complexity of the new nation would help to preserve. "Extend the sphere, and you take in a greater variety of parties and interests; you make it less probable that a majority of the whole will have a common motive to invade the rights of other citizens." However, as distances disappear and telecommunications shrink the sphere, and as the executive and legislative branches of government become more entwined with public opinion and popular demand, only the courts may be left to stand as an effective bastion against the tyranny of the majority. The judiciary, the branch of government that was designed to be the least responsive to popular passion, will bear an increasingly difficult and heavy burden to protect individual rights against popular assault.

Direct democracy, toward which we seem to be inexorably heading, was the earliest form of democracy, originating during the fifth century B.C. in the small, self-contained city-states of classical Greece. During the 200 years of Athenian direct democracy, the ancient city-state whose governance we know most about, a privileged few citizens served at one and the same time as both the rulers and the ruled, making and administering their own laws. "Although limited to adult males of native parentage," writes Donald Kagan, "Athenian citizenship granted full and active participation in every decision of the state without regard to wealth or class." Democracy in Athens was carried as far as it would go until modern times.

By contrast, representative government—democracy's second transformation—is a relatively recent phenomenon, originating in the United States a little more than two centuries ago. Under representative democracy, Americans—at first a privileged few and now every citizen over age 18—can vote for those who make the laws that govern them. Unlike the ancient Greeks, our Constitution specifies a government that separates the rulers from the ruled. It connects people to the government by elections, but distances the government from the people by making the elected the ones who actually enact the laws and conduct the business of government. As political scientist Harvey C. Mansfield put it, that "Constitutional space is the genius of American republicanism. It keeps the process of democratization under control and prevents our democracy from ruining itself by carrying itself to an extreme."

Today, that Constitutional space is shrinking. New populist processes and telecommunications technologies amplify the voice of the people at large and bring the public right back into the middle of the decision making processes of government. As the power of public opinion rises, the roles of the traditional political intermediaries—the parties, the mass media experts, and the governing elite—decline. Institutions that obstruct the popular will or stand between it and the actions of government get bypassed.

Telecommunications technologies—computers, satellites, interactive television, telephones and radio—are breaking down the age-old barriers of time and distance that originally precluded the nation's people from voting directly for the laws and policies that govern them. The general belief holds that representative government is the only form of democracy that is feasible in today's sprawling, heterogeneous nation-states. However, interactive telecommunications now make it possible for tens of millions of widely dispersed citizens to receive the information they need to carry out the business of government themselves, gain admission to the political realm, and retrieve at least some of the power over their own lives and goods that many believe their elected leaders are squandering.

The electronic republic, therefore, has already started to redefine the roles of citizenship and political leadership. Today, it is at least as important to reach out to the electorate—the public-at-large—and lobby public opinion, as it is to lobby the elect—the public officials who make the laws and administer the policies. In the words of literary critic Sven Birkerts in *The Gutenberg Elegies,* "The advent of the computer and the astonishing sophistication achieved by our electronic communications media have together turned a range of isolated changes into something systematic. The way that people experience the world has altered more in the last fifty years than in the many centuries preceding ours." The emergence of the electronic republic gives rise to the need for new thinking, new procedures, new policies, and even new political institutions to ensure that in the century ahead majoritarian impulses will not come at the expense of the rights of individuals and unpopular minorities.

We need to recognize the remarkable changes that the interactive telecommunications age is producing in our political system. We need to understand the consequences of the march toward democratization. We need to deal with the promise and perils of the electronic republic.

It can make government intensely responsive to the people. It also can carry responsiveness to an extreme, opening the way for manipulation, demagoguery or tyranny of the majority that, in the words of *The Federalist Papers,* "kindle[s] a flame . . . [and] spread[s] a general conflagration through the . . . States."

Most studies of government, politics, and the media start at the top by examining the qualities of leadership that define political life. However, in the coming era, the qualities of citizenship will be at least as important as those of political leadership. In an electronic republic, it will be essential to look at politics from the bottom up as well as from the top down.

What will it take to turn the United States into a nation of qualified citizens who are engaged not as isolated individuals pursuing their own ends but as public-spirited members who are dedicated to the common good? In an electronic republic, finding the answer to that question is essential. In the words of Thomas Jefferson, "I know no safe depository of the ultimate powers of the society but the people themselves, and if we think them not enlightened enough to exercise their control with a wholesome discretion, the remedy is not to take it from them, but to inform their discretion."

Lawrence K. Grossman, a 1989–90 Media Studies Center senior fellow, is the former president of PBS and NBC News and is currently president of the PBS Horizons Cable Network. This chapter is excerpted from his book, The Electronic Republic: Reshaping Democracy in the Information Age *(Viking, 1995).*

23

Town Hall On-Line

Sara B. Ivry

On-line communication is transforming interaction among media elites, politicians and citizens. In the 1994 mid-term elections, computer-based media initiatives at the national and local levels offered alternative channels for campaigning, lobbying and discussion; now they are being used to offer new means of education. Citizens can log onto a computer and learn about political candidates and organizations, about bills in Congress and grass-roots activity.

Fears that on-line media will render obsolete traditional forms of communication are unrealistic. Computers are not taking over. Rather, as demonstrated in 1994, computer-based media will complement traditional forms of communication to improve democracy and create a system of political communication that engages all sectors of society.

In 1994, politicians such as Dianne Feinstein, Ted Kennedy, Pete Wilson and Kathleen Brown made their platforms available on-line. "Thomas," a brainchild of the Library of Congress that has been widely touted by House Speaker Newt Gingrich, aims to put on-line all legislation considered and passed by Congress. The White House has its own home page on the World Wide Web, along with the CIA, FBI and many other agencies. Such data banks contain standard government information, and they are being used with growing frequency. A survey conducted at the MIT Artificial Intelligence Lab for the White House in January 1994 found that some 30,000–40,000 users were downloading documents daily. Some 65 percent of these users stated that electronic access to information allows for a more direct view of the political process.

Estimates suggest that by 1996, 35 million U.S. households will contain personal computers; 22 million of those computers will have modems enabling their users to log on to the Internet. Worldwide there are expected to be some 40 million Internet users, with 14 million of them in the United States—more than twice the estimate for Internet users in 1994.

In the United States, Internet users are not exactly heterogeneous. A 1994 survey in *WIRED,* whose conclusions were supported in a study conducted by MIT and the White House, found that 80 percent of Internet users are male and Caucasian; their median age is 31 and their median income is between $40,000 and $60,000.

Nevertheless, the Internet is fertile ground for grass-roots communications. Independent talk groups, which function less as data banks than as sites where individuals express their opinions, discuss everything from American foreign policy to euthanasia.

The Minnesota Electronic Democracy Project is a key example of an initiative which employed on-line media at a level between the elite and the grass roots. The project maintained two programs last fall. The first was an on-line debate between both gubernatorial and senatorial candidates. Both sets of candidates received three questions on three different dates leading up to the election; responses were posted to all project subscribers. Candidates were also given the opportunity to rebut their opponents. The project's second program was a discussion group open to all subscribed individuals. (Subscriptions were free to all who filed an E-mail request.) Participants discussed the candidates, negative political advertising and the relative importance of actually voting. In general, their statements were insightful and knowledgeable. The forum was especially valuable to candidates from small parties, who find it difficult to reach the general public. On days leading up to the election, according to mediator Scott Aikens, some 700 subscribers logged on to follow the debate. In addition, the debate received some 25,000 "hits"—times accessed—through other computer-based media access sites.

Similar projects abound. Harvard University student Mark Bonchek initiated the Political Participation Project—a one-stop gateway for a vast network of information concerning politics, lobby groups and non-profits. His project, which began in October 1994, is primarily an educational reference tool and sign post. It received some 825 hits during the week preceding the election. In the week following, that number fell to 769. Yet even in December, the project was receiving 170 hits a week, roughly 20–25 hits a day. Bonchek's hope is that this kind of initiative will serve as a "one-stop shop" where individuals can learn easily about politics without the traditional mediation of journalists.

The League of Women Voters has already taken steps to make access more widespread via its Wired for Democracy Project. Part of this program has installed public computers in libraries in four test-site cities, used by 4,000 people during the project's first 10 days. Similarly, the California Voter Foundation has installed some 177 computer terminals in 19 school libraries designed to teach students about the electoral process. Project Vote Smart, a California-based educational initiative, includes an on-line service which contained the biographies of the 2,000 federal candidates running in 1994.

These tools will not supplant traditional methods of education or communication. They will, instead, complement them. On-line services could enable a greater realization of principles like equal access to information and freedom of expression, both of which are commonly associated with a sound democracy.

Sara B. Ivry is a research assistant at the Edward R. Murrow Center for International Communication at the Fletcher School of Law and Diplomacy at Tufts University.

24

Journalism and the Internet

Andrew C. Gordon

It is a profound irony of our age: An explosion in the number and reach of communications media is coupled with widespread consternation at the shallowness of our public discourse. Traditional journalists worry about loss of readership and an apparent dampening in public respect. Yet one emerging electronic arena of communication, the Internet, is doubling in numbers of users every six months and fostering entirely new forms of public conversation. By responding effectively to the potential of this network of networks, journalists can recapture the high ground, reassert their standards and raise the level of public dialogue on complex issues.

The Internet is a worldwide network of computer networks that began as a Department of Defense-sponsored maze of links among a few massive research computers across the United States. Initially users had to own expensive computer equipment and dedicated phone lines, and had to be experts in arcane computer terminology to utilize the system.

But the system has been markedly simplified, and rigid text formats have given way to richer text and the inclusion of pictures, sound and animation. Breakthroughs in hardware and software enable users to connect to the Internet with moderately priced computers (less than $1,000) over existing phone lines. The experience of using computers has changed profoundly enough to escalate the numbers of users and providers. The Internet currently connects 40,000 networks and millions of users.

The most significant and relevant recent Internet development is the availability of point-and-click Hypertext browsers. Hypertext allows publishers to connect various types of information in a non-linear fashion. If this paragraph were presented in hypertext format, an interested reader could use a computer mouse to point to any of these underlined words, click on and "link" to another paragraph where Internet and Hypertext and Browser would be explained in more detail.

In Hypertext environments, it is as easy to link across the world as it is to link within an article. And from any link location one can easily link to another. But the glory of this capacity—instant access to varieties of information in any location—is also its Achilles' Heel.

In the example of this article you were invited to link to another location still within this article and subject to the same editorial control. But so much information is available in so many places—and so much of it is of highly variable quality—that the user is often lost in hyperspace. All of this creates new opportunities for reporters. Journalists, who are experienced with dealing with massive amounts of chaotic information and organizing it into a manageable form, have well-honed strategies for finding and dealing with sources, and for deciding *what* should be presented and *how*. These skills are desperately needed in the electronic world of the Internet, where users are awash in locations and sources.

No matter how scrupulously maintained the initial starting point, the cybernaut may be linked to sites containing information which is hopelessly out of date, half-baked, insensitively written or just plain wrong. Many popular sites are maintained by volunteers, transient graduate students, people lacking the resources or initiative to bring information up to date, or individuals who are strongly biased on important issues. Easy access to a wealth of information promotes a flowering of democratic ideals, but users are often hopelessly confused about which information has been subject to cross-checking and scrutiny.

Even if information is correct in its original setting, at many sites it may be wrenched out of the context within which it is meaningful or interpretable. My first encounter with this crucial issue occurred during a project to enable community organizations to tap into the City of Chicago's housing database. City officials used the database to create an aggregate picture of housing patterns in the city, including ownership of properties and parcels. Community organizations wanted to identify and act against the owners of particular slum property. From the city's perspective the data were good enough to depict typical aggregate use. But because of the dynamics of housing ownership, the data about any *particular* property might be in error. When city officials with experience in encountering these inevitable inaccuracies acted against a slumlord, they would treat the database as only one source among many. They would augment the information in the database with the results of research procedures such as up-to-date title searches and histories of previous legal actions. Data which were entirely sufficient for one purpose were wholly insufficient for another, however, and to interpret this merely as a problem of errors in data is to oversimplify vastly the contextual nature of information collection and interpretation.

In a similar way, the Internet presents users with assertions wrenched out of context. But the Internet and Hypertext offer solutions to this problem and enhancements to journalistic practice as well.

Reporters often express frustration at the limitations of their traditional formats when they wish to present complex and important matters. Yet at a recent Freedom Forum conference, Lord Asa Briggs, author of a history of the BBC, urged responsible journalists to help citizens understand the *complexity* of events rather than their simplicity. How can journalists reconcile the constraints of their craft and Lord Briggs' suggestion? Rather than worrying about the worst excesses of the new media, or succumbing to its glitzy features, journalists can embrace the Internet in a way which elevates the profession by following Lord Briggs' advice. A sensible deployment of the Internet can allow journalists to transcend the limitations of current technologies and help readers to find more contextual information.

Properly implemented, Hypertext links could provide useful background for novice readers, glossaries to unusual terms, and, for those seeking it, technical detail. Links could be made to earlier stories about the same or similar issues in the same journal. Edward Tufte, author of important books on the effective presentation of quantitative information, reminds us that the analytic question is always "compared to what?" Relevant comparisons are always useful and normally inaccessible to readers interpreting political events.

Yet as the Bosnian crisis evolves, for example, journalists on the Internet could incorporate Hypertext links to the history of such regional clashes. Or as welfare reform is debated, links could invite the readers to consider the welfare experience from the perspective of recent recipients. As the election season heats up, links could be made to information about likely or disaffected voters in various regions. When the next child welfare tragedy erupts, links could already have been prepared to descriptions of similar crises in other jurisdictions or eras. These links, prepared by journalists, would direct attention to endemic issues instead of emphasizing single-mindedly the failings of current administrators.

Some news outlets (the *Seattle Times,* for example) are experimenting with the potential of these new forms. And the New Century Network, whose formation was announced in April 1995, will bring together 123 daily newspapers from Advance Publications, Inc., Cox Newspapers, Inc., the Gannett Company, the Hearst Corporation, Knight-Ridder, Inc., the Times Mirror Company, the Tribune Company and the Washington Post Company—to create common standards for electronic publishing on the Internet.

Journalists can build on recent models to enrich the context for interpretation and understanding in another way. Hundreds of publishers (*Time,* the *San Jose Mercury News*), businesses, governmental sources, libraries, museums, schools, universities and students in their dorm rooms have developed home pages (assemblies of text, graphics and links) accessible worldwide from their individual computers. Reporters should see such early ventures into cyberspace as ways to use their skills at research, reporting and analysis in new locations. Rather than dismiss new media as interlopers, journalists should seize the opportunities they provide to enrich and to extend the best of journalistic practice.

Andrew C. Gordon is a professor in the Graduate School of Public Affairs and adjunct professor in the School of Communications at the University of Washington.

25

Hyde Park on Television

Dirk Smillie

Scenes from Toronto television: A young man in a T-shirt protesting a rise in fuel prices holds up three gas-company credit cards and says, "I've got to say to you, Canadian Tire, Esso, Petro-Canada, if this doesn't stop, these cards get cut up." A week later, gas prices have gone even higher. He returns to the camera with bad news for the gas companies: "Damn! . . . That's criminal. Have you no shame? So, I made the vow, and that's right. . . ." Gleefully he cuts the three cards in half with scissors.

Welcome to "Speakers Corner," the show that originates out of video kiosks which record messages from random visitors, that are in turn broadcast by Citytv, an independent television station that serves Toronto and much of southern Ontario. Citytv, founded in 1972 by Moses Znaimer, is dedicated to spontaneous and interactive television. That dedication reaches its fullest expression through "Speakers Corner," which functions as a cross between a church confessional and an amusement-park photo booth.

Essentially, "Speakers Corner," which first appeared in 1989, involves a small enclosure that houses a video camera trained on a seat. For $1 Canadian, a patron gets two minutes of uninterrupted time on-camera. All proceeds from the video soapbox go to a Canadian charity for children.

The original kiosk is open 24 hours a day and has been visited by everyone from drunken newlyweds and hockey fans to the leader of the Canadian Conservative Party. Most visitors, however, are the young and the rambunctious. As a 1994 newspaper article noted, the kiosk with the camera is often a place "where the loaded come to unload."

"Speakers Corner" has both its champions and critics. Antonia Zerbisian, television critic for the *Toronto Star,* calls the video-kiosk broadcasts "truly democratic," because they reflect Toronto's melting-pot demographics. "In a television universe where we're so used to seeing the same magic rolodex of experts every day," she says, "it's wonderful to have these other points of view."

Toronto Star pop critic Peter Howell disagrees, arguing that what passes for other points of view includes inebriated nightclub patrons disgorging on-screen. "Every day," said Howell, "you have people exposing themselves and a lot of visits by the (accused Oklahoma City bomber) Tim McVeighs of the world."

True, "Speakers Corner" has "a fair amount of hijinks," says Znaimer. "It's a rough and real alternative" to the "slick, prepackaged" media content of its lumbering neighbor to the south, he says, observing that the key to its success is its "unmediated" character. Beyond the video flotsam and jetsam come such segments as pleas for information on lost family pets, marriage proposals and a debate on the Canadian cigarette tax. So far, the most controversial scene to air was a visit by two attractive young women who discussed AIDS prevention as they unrolled a condom on a banana. The segment "lit up the wires" with protest, says "Speakers Corner" editor Paula Virany.

To Znaimer, "Speakers Corner" is one of Citytv's most enduring innovations and the first successful television version of letters to the editor. Of the hundreds of segments taped by patrons each week, Virany estimates that a little over 10 percent make it onto the air—usually in an edited form. Although the ratio may seem small, it is actually larger than that typical of letters to the editor printed by a daily newspaper: The *New York Times,* by comparison, estimates that of the 75,000 letters a year it receives only about 3,000, or 4 percent, appear in print.

"Speakers Corner" draws an audience of about 100,000 viewers each weekend, with a large following among 18–to-34–year-olds, says Jay Switzer, vice president for programming at CHUM television, the parent company of Citytv. Demand on "Speakers Corner" booths has risen steadily during six years of operation, says Znaimer, who estimates that on average 1,000 to 1,500 patrons visit the booths each week.

Portable versions of "Speakers Corner" are now found at more than a half-dozen locations around Canada and as far south as Buenos Aires, Argentina. The kiosks have appeared at bar mitzvahs, Earth Day festivals and political conventions. Znaimer says that more are on the way.

Dirk Smillie writes on media for the Christian Science Monitor *and other publications. He was a staff member at the Media Studies Center for several years.*

V

Books

26

Sounding the Alarm

Christopher Dornan

The Electronic Commonwealth:
The Impact of New Media Technologies on Democratic Politics
by Jeffrey B. Abramson, F. Christopher Arterton
and Gary R. Orren.
New York: Basic Books, 1988.

The Media and Democracy
by John Keane
Cambridge, Mass.: Blackwell Publishers, 1991.

The Roar of the Crowd:
How Television and People Power are Changing the World
by Michael J. O'Neill
New York: Times Books, 1993.

Information Society and Civil Society:
Contemporary Perspectives on the Changing World Order
Edited by Slavko Splichal, Andrew Calabrese
and Colin Sparks.
West Lafayette, Ind.: Purdue University Press, 1994.

Communication and Democracy
Edited by Slavko Splichal and Janet Wasko
Norwood, N.J.: Ablex Publishing Corporation, 1993.

Read All About It!
The Corporate Takeover of America's Newspapers
by James D. Squires
New York: Times Books, 1993.

The New News v. *The Old News:*
The Press and Politics in the 1990s
Essays by Jay Rosen and Paul Taylor
New York: Twentieth Century Fund Press, 1992.

The People's Right to Know:
Media, Democracy, and the Information Highway
Edited by Frederick Williams and John V. Pavlik
Hillsdale, N.J.: Lawrence Erlbaum Associates, 1994

As usual, Auden put his finger on it. In "Epistle to a Godson," a poem written toward the end of his life for Philip Spender, he delivers a boozy state-of-the-world address and says aloud what they both know:

> *. . . You don't need me to tell you what's*
> *going on: the ochlocratic media,*
> *   joint with under-the-dryer gossip,*
> *   process and vent without intermission*
>
> *all today's ugly secrets. Imageable*
> *no longer, a featureless anonymous*
> *   threat from behind, to-morrow has us*
> *   gallowed shitless...*

Writing more than a decade before the spectacles of Oprah and O.J. came to rule the airwaves, Auden was able to spot the media processing and venting "all today's ugly secrets"; and to recognize that when one lives on a diet of gossip and calamity, the future becomes impossible to imagine except as an oncoming disaster. Things will only continue to get worse. Still, there is nothing startling about the complaint that the rise of media culture has cheapened and degraded public life and eviscerated democratic discourse; this has all but enshrined itself as a truism. But as Clive James pointed out in 1973, shortly after the poem appeared, it is how Auden states the case.

The poet writes: "...the media, joint with under-the-dryer gossip..." He means "...*together* with under-the-dryer gossip..." but he chose to use an archaic form. He says the future "has us gallowed shitless." It is an evocative image and the meaning is obvious, but he chose the verb to gallow, which is an obsolete form of to frighten. He describes the media as ochlocratic, which is a word you never hear the media use, because it's the sort of word you have to look up. It means ruled by the mob.

Auden is writing in forgotten words. One of the things the media have done, the composition insists, is to constrict the sphere of what can be said in public so as to annihilate an entire echelon of discourse. We lose the ability to converse with ourselves at a certain pitch. Instead, public discussion becomes a dialogue of limited vocabulary and penny-ante ideas. And we lose the ability to understand, much less appreciate, the poetry of Auden.

This is central to the discourse of alarm that attends discussions of the contemporary mass media (and democracy). It is shared, as John Keane points out in *The Media and Democracy*, by both right and left. The right inherit it from the elitist disdain of T.S. Eliot and others, while the left follow lines of denunciation laid down by Theodor Adorno and Max Horkheimer, who saw "the culture industry" as a giant mechanism whereby public thought was commodified and lobotomized into "stylized barbarism." The complaint is not simply that these enormous agencies of public address are being squandered on trivia and titillation when they could well be instruments of social betterment. Rather, as almost everyone who thinks seriously about the matter agrees, it's that they are actively making us all dumber. Right and left differ only on whether this is inadvertent or structurally convenient.

As the media come to dominate public life, so the complaint runs, their values become society's values. But the media's values are entirely inappropriate to the conduct of a thinking and caring collective, because the media's values are superficiality and histrionics, opportunism and the fast buck. They are therefore implicated—if not indeed the usual prime suspects—in what is universally perceived to be a tight downward spiral in the quality of intellectual, cultural and political life.

So it has become all but mandatory to castigate the media. The chief sin, at least of the American media, is also their chief selling point—namely that what the market demands and what they promise in return is relentless, effortless, transient gratification. In a word, fun. There is nothing wrong with pleasant diversion, except when it supersedes what it was supposed to be a diversion from. Myriad pleasures are neither effortless nor transient: the satisfaction of a demanding job well done, the joy of parenthood's unforgiving duties, or the rewards of civic responsibility. But a society whose highest aspiration is perpetual amusement surely devalues other forms of accomplishment and satisfaction. As Robert Warshow put it in *The Partisan Review* in 1948, "euphoria spreads over our culture like the broad smile of an idiot."

Far from being bulwarks of democracy, the media are roundly criticized as factors in its frustration. They corrupt politics, not only because their preoccupation with "image" smothers substantive policy debates, but because their volatile interest in the private lives of public figures scares most sane people away from running for office, leaving only the deluded and the megalomaniacal. Even more damaging, they have throttled the full expression of debate, narrowing public attention to referendums on charisma—a quality the media themselves confer and revoke—or to contests between campaign machines. If democracy has been reduced to a periodic plebiscite on one set of administrative managers over another, the media have compounded matters by ensuring that even these decisions will be driven by sentiment, not by the rigorous airing of arguments and ideas.

These are complaints Americans themselves make about American media culture. The complaints from countries on the receiving end of U.S. cultural exports are even more acid. The allure of American "fun" is irresistible, as is its purchase price, but the cost is said to be a surrender to Hollywood hegemony. When something as inconsequential as "The Brady Bunch" is dubbed into multiple languages, something consequential is afoot. CNN beamed the anguish in Oklahoma City live for days on end to Lisbon and Melbourne and Rio, but if it had happened in Lisbon or Melbourne or Rio, would CNN have broken stride? No. Only because it was an American tragedy was the world invited to grieve.

In one way or another, then, each of these books condemns the current media order. But together they also sound an alarm of new urgency. Three related developments animate this latest barrage of concern.

The first is the widely-held perception that the general conduct of the media—hardly admired in the first place—is rapidly deteriorating right before our eyes. This is difficult to contest. Ten years ago, the respectable press did not use a supermarket tabloid as its stalking horse on sex-scandal allegations about a presidential candidate; the defining news stories of the moment did not feature in quick succession a pop idol accused of child molestation, a woman who cut off her husband's penis, a figure skater who arranged an assault on a rival, and a former football great accused of murder. The complaint is not that a tabloid sensibility exists, but that its norms have become rudely ascendant.

Secondly, there is the recognition that new technologies—and new alignments of corporate interest—are rewiring the switchboard of public communication. Once-dominant media institutions are being joined by cable, satellites, fiber optics and networked computers. In huge sectors of the cultural industries, media ownership has reached the global level. Lines of nationalism and identity are being redrawn, in no small part because of the new communication technologies. All of this both renews the threat to democracy and holds the promise of redemption.

Thirdly, as both *The Roar of the Crowd* and a number of the contributors to *Communication and Democracy* point out, there is the challenge presented by the collapse of communist rule—a development in which mass communication is implicated. Exposure to Western media stoked the dissatisfaction of citizens in the East with the conditions under which they lived, while the popular revolutions that brought down the Soviet bloc would not have been possible without access to means of communication. But toppling an authoritarian order does not guarantee a transition to democracy, and the new circumstances of the Soviet successor states make the West's disquiet with its own media all the more poignant. If the nations of Central and Eastern Europe are to become true democracies, they must overhaul their formerly state-controlled media, since free media are essential to a free society. But how should that be done? The West, it seems, has little to offer by way of example, except perhaps a lesson in what to avoid.

All these works therefore call for corrective measures. Free media are essential to a free society, and the task is to recapture the conditions under which they can function as such. In the Western media, the discourse of alarm cohabits with an equally insistent discourse of congratulation, in which the media are routinely lauded as crucial to Western liberty.

The traditional textbook history of the press provides the best example of this congratulatory account. As a machine for the mass replication of texts, the printing press made possible the circulation of ideas and arguments to a vast, dispersed public, setting in motion the circumstances whereby the will of such a public might become a decisive factor on the political stage. In addition, because it was mobile and relatively easy to conceal, the printing press proved to be notoriously difficult for traditional authorities to control. The result was a new politics that allowed the governed a voice in determining how they were ruled. Print made possible a public discourse on human affairs that would provide the foundation for democratic systems: the recognition that the course of events might be influenced by publicly commenting on them. It demonstrated that democracy does not consist purely of a universal franchise exercised periodically at the polling booth. It exists in the unbridled welter of public argument and opinion on the issues of the day. Without the latter, the former is empty and illusory. Hence, it is not simply that a democratic society tolerates a free press, but that a free press makes for a democratic society.

By historical precedent and philosophical principle, then, under liberal democracy no political agency should be hierarchically dominant over public expression. It is precisely this freedom from external constraint that ostensibly allows the media to police the conduct of other social institutions and authorities. And given that democracy is anchored in public dialogue, any attempt to inhibit that discourse is anathema, since control over public debate would amount to control over the political process itself.

The dilemma faced by those who call for reform of current media practice is therefore obvious and obstinate. The mechanism that has historically guaranteed the independence of public communication is the market: by earning its livelihood from the patronage of paying customers, the Fourth Estate is beholden to no warrant save popular will. But it is the logic of the market that has supposedly led to the dysfunctions of the present situation, in which mass communication has become the preserve of a small number of gargantuan corporate enterprises and the media have all but abrogated the civic responsibilities they once claimed justified their strict autonomy. Redrafting the rules by which public communication should be conducted would therefore require intervening in the affairs of the media market, but the only social institution with the authority to do so is the state, and the media cannot be subject to the dictates of the state without violating a fundamental tenet of liberal democracy. The conundrum is a classic double-bind: democracy can only be redeemed by its own betrayal.

With the prominent exception of the United States, most Western democracies have long accepted that the imperatives of the market are not perfectly coincident with those of the public good, at least in matters of mass communication. Accordingly, they have attempted to compensate by establishing traditions of public broadcasting, in which taxpayer-supported networks provide programming that the private sector either cannot or will not. Free from state interference, organizations such as the BBC and the CBC are expected to coexist with private broadcasters in a mixed system, in which each element forestalls the potential deficiencies of the other. The private sector is supposed to prevent the public from becoming too elitist, while the public sector prevents the private from becoming too vulgar.

However, as Keane points out, even this compromise is in jeopardy. As channels proliferate, the hold of the public broadcasters on audiences diminishes. As their audiences dwindle while national deficits mount, their sizeable government grants come to be seen as extravagances that are increasingly difficult to justify. In an effort to reclaim audiences they often ape the programming of the private sector, which only undermines their *raison d'etre*. Everywhere in the West the future of public broadcasting is clouded, adding another element to the climate of anxiety.

What, then, is to be done? Broadly, these books propose three avenues of recourse. One, shared by *The Roar of the Crowd, Read all About It!* and *The New News* v. *The Old News,* is classically liberal in its faith that just pronouncing on the way things are can influence the way things should be. By sounding a plangent hue and cry, surely something will be done.

These three volumes represent the work of four authors—three journalists and one professor of journalism. Uniformly, their contributions are informative, thoughtful and a pleasure to read. Still, they tend to rehearse obvious arguments as though these were new and they rely on tales from the trenches to tell the story of the entire war. Their strength lies in their documentation of what is amiss, rather than what to do about it.

For example, in *The Roar of the Crowd,* Michael J. O'Neill, former editor of the New York *Daily News,* recites the most astonishing episodes of the past few years whenever mass communication has met power politics. His account of Yeltsin's defeat of the 1991 Soviet *coup* is worth the purchase price alone. But in the end the book is more an almanac than a treatise. Similarly, in *Read All About It!,* James D. Squires, former editor of the *Chicago Tribune,* decries what he sees as the corruption of journalistic ideals by the crass interests of profit. He tells the story deftly, with a former insider's lust to spill the beans and a lifelong journalist's eye for detail. (In Squires' day as a reporter, for example, the desire to separate journalistic church and state meant that business and editorial employees at the *Tribune* were required to take separate elevators.) It's a good yarn. The argument, however, is unconvincing. To these admittedly younger eyes, it is not clear that corporate control of the media rather than control by megalomaniacal ideologues is any great loss. And while Squires sees the separate elevators as a symbol of the proper independence of the editorial division from the influence of advertising and circulation, they can equally be seen as a ploy to keep the paper's journalists in the dark about the business end of their livelihood. If the traditions of American journalism are under assault, Squires offers no structural solution. He trusts that thoughtful men and women within the ranks of journalism, once alerted to the crisis, will be galvanized into resisting the corporate managers. Alas, this is a dubious prospect. As long ago as 1947, the Hutchins Commission on Freedom of the Press averred that "there are some things which a truly professional man will not do for money." Events would seem to have shown otherwise.

The New News v. *The Old News* collects two essays, one by Jay Rosen, an associate professor of journalism at New York University, and the other by Paul Taylor, a former reporter at the *Washington Post* and the author of *See How They Run.* Both embark from the proposition that something ugly has happened to political journalism. They are both impassioned, intelligent and engaged, but they still peter out when it comes to a program for reform. Taylor's suggestions culminate in the recommendation that a little more unmediated access to the electorate for politicians might be helpful, in the form of, say, nightly free-time five-minute broadcasts during presidential elections. Given the scope of the problem, this seems to be small change. Rosen, similarly, calls for an end to junk journalism through a reinvigoration of the enterprise according to a public agenda—namely that journalists should keep the public interest foremost in mind in the conduct of their work. The fact that journalists apparently need to be reminded that theirs is a labor performed in the public service is revealing in itself, but the avenue of redress is curiously unsatisfying. Although the problem with the media is located at the structural level—in the fact that they are governed by ineluctable market economics—the solution is to be found by playing on the consciences of individual journalists, who are enjoined to alter their comportment. The faith in the power of mere individuals to effect structural change is admirable, but no sign of a wholesale mutiny against current media practice has been forthcoming.

The other books are by academics, and so the consciences of working journalists don't count for much either way. In this narrative universe, agency is circumscribed by structure—at least the agency of media-conglomerate employees.

With that in common, the academic volumes can be divided themselves into two camps. *The Electronic Commonwealth, The People's Right to Know* and *The Media and Democracy* can be grouped by virtue of their objects of attention and their relative accessibility. The anthologies *Communication and Democracy* and *Information Society and Civil Society* are steeped in a more rarified debate, and hence make no bid for a wide audience.

Keane's *The Media and Democracy* takes the historical view, charting a course into the multimedia future by revisiting the writings of seminal political polemicists, from Milton to Mill. This would be a marvelous idea, if only it were better executed. What is supposed to be sweeping is too often halting, and the rereading of political theory leads to proposals that are unpersuasive. (In *Information Society and Civil Society*, Colin Sparks raises grave objections to Keane's earlier work in the theory of democracy.) *The People's Right to Know* and *The Electronic Commonwealth* look to the future and invest their faith in the new communication technologies. They argue much the same thing, except that the former reads like the noisy proceedings of a series of meetings, while the latter, although joint-authored, has the rhythm and coherence of a well-argued position.

The new technologies, these works contend, could break the hold of corporate communication and place the power of communication in the hands of the citizens and create new concourses of public interaction, information retrieval and exchange. However, they can just as easily become instruments of demagoguery rather than democracy, entrenching rather than loosening corporate and state control. Accordingly, measures must be taken—and taken now—to ensure that the new technologies develop with the best interests of the polity in mind. This will presumably require action on the part of the state, but this is forgiven on the grounds that, first, the motives are pure, and second, it does not entail state interference in existing media practice. Rather, it would involve merely setting the initial conditions from which the new technologies would take shape. *The People's Right to Know*, for example, proposes the creation of a publicly supported National Citizens' Information Service to prevent the infobahn from becoming the exclusive playground of profit. *The Electronic Commonwealth* urges similar action if only because "The marketplace itself is not likely to support electronic information services devoted to exchanges of civic information." Keane goes even further, championing a public service model of the communication future in which "politically accountable, supra-national regulatory bodies" would "'de-concentrate' and publicly regulate privately-owned media and restrict the scope and intensity of corporate speech."

These might be described as the soft and hard options with regard to the new technologies. Neither looks promising. Keane's view is not only unworkable (the United States, in particular, will never consent to supra-national regulation of private sector communication) but fraught with its own dangers. What he proposes smacks of censorship disguised as regulation, and therefore contravenes one of democracy's founding principles. He attempts to bully his way out of the double-bind simply by closing his eyes to the implications of his proposals. The soft option, while more palatable, seems no more likely. First, the United States does not have a strong tradition of this type of public-service endeavour, and second, the political will for such enterprises appears to be lacking even in those countries where the tradition exists.

In the volumes *Information Society and Civil Society* and *Communication and Democracy*, a number of scholars worry away at a third course, inspired by the concept of "civil society." The former is a collection of papers delivered at the Fourth International Colloquium on Communication and Culture, sponsored by the University of Ljubljana; the latter emerges from the 17th conference of the International Association for Mass Communication Research. The term "civil society" originally designated a social space apart from the state: a bourgeois realm of commerce, private property and individual rights, exempt from state administration and control. It is an especially attractive concept to intellectuals who lived under the former Soviet hegemony, in which there was no civil society: no equivalent of the Rotary Club, the church basement, the public square, except that permitted and organized by the state and the Communist party. In some quarters, the concept has been reworked to describe a social sphere separate from and untainted by both the state and corporate economy. It suggests a haven outside traditional structures of power for the conduct of political life—a space for truly democratic intercourse. In that regard, it offers a way out of the double-bind. Public communication should be answerable neither to the apparatus of the state nor to corporate control, but to a civil society (or its contemporary equivalent, the information society), where profit and power are neither the means nor the ends.

The arguments advanced in these two anthologies are complex and intriguing—excellent examples of intellectual discussion conducted at a pitch the popular media cannot accommodate—but like many of the preoccupations of the intelligentsia of the left, they seem over-theorized and under-realized. What they envision is a certain utopia, but the published proceedings of a couple of academic gatherings are unlikely to will this new world into being.

Where does this leave us? Apparently, back where we began, in a state of apprehended emergency. However, it is important to remember that there is nothing new in the worry that the media are damaging to democracy. It has its roots in the 19th century, as a concomitant of what this alarm is about, namely the rise of a truly *mass* commercial press. As early as 1902, the chancellor of Queen's University in Canada, Sir Sandford Fleming, alarmed at the state of the popular press, announced a $250–prize essay competition on the topic, "How can Canadian universities best benefit the profession of journalism, as a means of molding and elevating public opinion?"

The 13 entries, published in an anthology the following year, uniformly lamented that the press, unprecedented in its potential as "a popular educator and a moral force," was being squandered on the opposite: "It kills time, satisfies the thirst for scandal, and acts as a preventive to thought." Each of the essays deplored Canadian journalism's preoccupation with lurid crime, its invasions of privacy, the dominance of American content, the unsavory influence of advertising, the literary bankruptcy of newspaper prose, and the fact that reading matter had become "a 'rivulet of text' amid a wilderness of pictures." Indeed, in a strikingly modern passage, one W.S. Johnston of Montreal saw the popular papers as part of the degradation of the times, an era characterized by "exaggeration and artificiality," and chafed that "this 'froth and scum' of the world's news has demoralized our journalism; it threatens our modern culture like some new wave of barbarism....This is an age...of gradual decay, of obliteration of the highest ideals, of secularization—the beginning of a period of lapse—the end of a great period of history." Except for the telltale literacy, that passage could have been written yesterday.

There are two lessons one can take from the Queen's University essayists. The first is that the conduct of mass communication has always been accompanied by a running discourse of intellectual alarm that seeks to shame the media into behaving more responsibly. Ineffective though that discourse may seem, imagine what things might be like without it.

Secondly, although the Queen's University essays adopt an apocalyptic tone, in retrospect it was justified. In 1902, the world did stand on the brink of cataclysmic change, in which an old order would crumble in unimaginable violence. These eight books are the equivalent almost a century later: Their recommendations may not be perfectly satisfying, but they offer convincing evidence that we are in the midst of large-scale shifts in the means and content of public communication, and they make a necessary contribution to the dialogue on what to do about it.

Christopher Dornan is associate professor at the School of Journalism and Communication at Carleton University in Ottawa, Canada.

For Further Reading

Abramson, Jeffrey B., F. Christopher Arterton and Gary R. Orren. *The Electronic Commonwealth: The Impact of New Media Technologies on Democratic Politics.* New York: Basic Books, 1988.

Arterton, F. Christopher. *Teledemocracy: Can Technology Protect Democracy?* Newbury Park, Calif.: Sage Publications, 1987.

Baker, C. Edwin. *Advertising and a Democratic Press.* Princeton, N.J.: Princeton University Press, 1994.

Berman, Daniel K. *Words Like Colored Glass: The Role of the Press in Taiwan's Democratization Process.* Boulder, Colo.: Westview Press, 1992.

Budge, Ian and David McKay, eds. *Developing Democracy: Comparative Research in Honour of J.F.P. Blondel.* Thousand Oaks, Calif.: Sage Publications, 1994.

Chomsky, Noam. *Necessary Illusions: Thought Control in Democratic Societies.* Boston, Mass.: South End Press, 1989.

Cmiel, Kenneth. *Democratic Eloquence: The Fight Over Popular Speech in Nineteenth Century America.* New York: William Morrow, 1990.

Dennis, Everette E. and John C. Merrill. *Media Debates: Issues in Mass Communication.* New York: Longman, 1991.

Dennis, Everette E. and Robert W. Snyder, eds. *Media and Public Life.* New Brunswick, N.J.: Transaction Publishers, 1997.

Entman, Robert M. *Democracy Without Citizens: Media and the Decay of American Politics.* New York: Oxford University Press, 1989.

Grossman, Lawrence K. *The Electronic Republic: Reshaping Democracy in the Information Age.* New York: Viking, 1995.

Habermas, Jürgen. *The Structural Transformation of the Public Sphere: An Inquiry into a Category of Bourgeois Society.* Cambridge, Mass.: MIT Press, 1989.

Jamieson, Kathleen Hall. *Dirty Politics: Deception, Distraction, and Democracy.* New York: Oxford University Press, 1992.

Kaid, Lynda L., and Christina Holtz-Bacha. *Political Advertising in Western Democracies: Parties & Candidates on Television.* Thousand Oaks, Calif.: Sage Publications, 1995.

Keane, John. *The Media and Democracy.* Cambridge, Mass.: Blackwell Publishers, 1991.

Kellner, Douglas. *Television and the Crisis of Democracy.* Boulder, Colo.: Westview Press, 1990.

Kingsford-Smith, Dimity and Dawn Oliver. *Economical With the Truth: The Law and the Media in a Democratic Society.* Oxford: ESC Publishers, 1990.

Lanham, Richard A. *The Electronic Word: Democracy, Technology, and the Arts.* Chicago: University of Chicago Press, 1993.

Laufer, Romain and Catherine Paradeise. *Marketing Democracy: Public Opinion and Media Formation in Democratic Societies.* New Brunswick, N.J.: Transaction, 1990.

Lichtenberg, Judith, ed. *Democracy and the Mass Media: A Collection of Essays.* New York: Cambridge University Press, 1991.

Mazzocco, Dennis. *Networks of Power: Corporate TV's Threat to Democracy.* Boston, Mass.: South End Press, 1994.

McChesney, Robert W. *Telecommunications, Mass Media, and Democracy: The Battle for the Control of U.S. Broadcasting.* New York: Oxford University Press, 1993.

Merritt, Davis. *Public Journalism and Public Life: Why Telling the News is Not Enough.* Hillsdale, N.J.: Lawrence Erlbaum Associates, 1995.

O'Neill, Michael J. *Faster Than a Speeding Bullet: Mass Communications and the Chaos of Democracy.* New York: Times Books, 1992.

O'Neill, Michael J. *The Roar of the Crowd: How Television and People Power are Changing the World.* New York: Times Books, 1993.

Raboy, Marc and Peter A. Bruck, eds. *Communication: For & Against Democracy.* Montreal: Black Rose Books, 1989.

Raboy, Marc and Bernard Dagenais. *Media, Crisis and Democracy: Mass Communication and the Disruption of Social Order.* Newbury Park, Calif.: Sage Publications, 1992.

Rosen, Jay and Paul Taylor. *The New News* v. *The Old News: The Press and Politics in the 1990s.* New York: Twentieth Century Fund Press, 1992.

Rothman, Stanley, ed. *The Mass Media in Liberal Democratic Societies.* New York: Paragon House, 1991.

Rubin, Bernard. *Media, Politics, and Democracy.* New York: Oxford University Press, 1977.

Schmuhl, Robert. *Demanding Democracy.* Notre Dame: University of Notre Dame Press, 1994.

Schudson, Michael. *The Power of News.* Cambridge, Mass.: Harvard University Press, 1995.

Splichal, Slavko, Andrew Calabrese and Colin Sparks, eds. *Information Society and Civil Society: Contemporary Perspectives on the Changing World Order.* West Lafayette, Ind.: Purdue University Press, 1994.

Splichal, Slavko and Janet Wasko, eds. *Communication and Democracy.* Norwood, N.J.: Ablex Publishing Corporation, 1993.

Squires, James D. *Read All About It!: The Corporate Takeover of America's Newspapers.* New York: Times Books, 1993.

Williams, Frederick and John V. Pavlik, eds. *The People's Right to Know: Media, Democracy, and the Information Highway.* Hillsdale, N.J.: Lawrence Erlbaum Associates, 1994.

Index

Minnesota Electronic Democracy
  Project, 166
and niche marketing, 135, 136, 137–
  38, 139, 140
and opinion journalism, 115
Political Participation Project
  (Harvard), 166–67
Project Vote Smart (California), 167
"Speakers Corner" (Canada), 173–75
"Thomas" (Library of Congress),
  165
Wired for Democracy Project
  (League of Women Voters),
  167
See also Internet
Internet
demographics of users, 166
development of, 169
Hypertext, 170–72
information credibility, 170–71
and inherent democratic role of
  media, 10–11
New Century Network, 172
Iran
government censorship in, 75–76
politics-media relationship in, 6

Japan, historical journalism and, 131–
  33
Jewish Holocaust, historical journalism
  and, 128, 129, 130–31, 132–33
Journalism vs. economics
and advertising revenue, 144, 146
and credibility, 145–47
and democracy, 143, 146, 147
and First Amendment ideology, 143,
  144, 147
news defined, 143
news products defined, 144–45
and professionalism, 144, 145–47
and public education, 143, 146
readers defined, 143
See also Market economies; Niche
  marketing
Journalism vs. media
and commercialism, 102–4, 105
competition between, 102–4
and credibility, 99, 102–3, 106
and democracy, 101, 104, 105–6
influence of cable television, 101–2
influence of interactive telecommu-

nications, 102
and media diversity, 99–101
and reduction in print literacy, 104–5
Journalistic practice
objectivity
  and credibility, 151–53
  and opinion journalism, 115–16
responsibility
  and historical journalism, 127–29,
    131–33
  and Poland, 71–72, 74
  and political leadership images,
    108–9
topic coverage
  comprehensive, 24
  intellectual, 23–24
  universal, 24
See also Credibility, journalistic;
  Historical journalism; Niche
  marketing; Opinion journalism;
  Political leadership, journalistic
  images of; Public journalism

Kazakhstan, 81
Keane, John, 179, 181, 185, 187, 188

Latin America
Argentina, 59, 62, 63, 64, 65
Brazil, 59, 61, 62, 63, 64, 65
cable television in, 64–65
Chile, 60, 62–63, 65
Colombia, 59, 60
democracy in, 59, 62, 63
government censorship in, 59, 60, 62
journalistic practice in, 59
  and corruption, 63–64
  credibility of, 61–62, 63–64
  licensing for, 60–61
market economy of, 65
Peru, 60, 61
politics-media relationship in, 61–63
Uruguay, 61, 65
Venezuela, 60–62, 63, 64
LatinoNet, 137
Lebanon
media assistance from United States,
  90
politics-media relationship in, 6
Licensing, media (Latin America), 60–
  61